# GOD FIRST
## IS THE
# KEY
## TO
# SUCCESS

MEDICINE TO THE WORLD
INSPIRATIONAL MESSAGES

OSVALDO R BURGOS JR.

Copyright © 2024 Osvaldo R Burgos Jr..

All rights reserved.

No part of this publication may be reproduced, distributed or transmitted in any form or by any means, including photocopying, recording or other electronic or mechanical methods, without the prior written permission of the publisher, except in the case of brief quotations, reviews and other noncommercial uses permitted by copyright law.

# Contents

**Introduction** .............................. xv
- Success Beyond the Surface ............... xvi
- Biblical Examples of Success............. xviii
- A Foundation Built on God ............... xix
- The Uncertainties of Life................. xxi
- Family Success: Joshua's Example ......... xxii
- Can We Build a Successful Life Without God?................................... xxiii
- The Pitfalls of Success Without God ....... xxiii
- The Example of Isaac's Obedience to God ...xxv
- Worldly Success Versus God-Given Success xxvi
- The Foundation of True Success.......... xxvii

**Chapter 1. Faith and Trust**.................... 1
- The Power of Faith and Trust in God ..........1
- The Foundation of Faith .....................3

- Understanding God's Sovereignty ........3
- Faith as a Life Force ....................4
- The Importance of Trust ...............4
- Hebrews 11:6: A Faithful Life Pleases God ..5
- The Reward of Faithful Trust ...........6
• The Story of Abraham: Faith Against the Odds ..6
  - The Call to Leave the Comfort Zone (Genesis 12:1) .......................7
  - God's Promises and Abraham's Faith (Genesis 12:2) .......................7
  - Abraham's Material Success (Genesis 13:2)..8
  - Trusting God with Personal Challenges (Hebrews 11:6) .......................9
  - The Journey of Faith: Lessons for Our Lives ...................................10
• Hannah's Story: Faith in Adversity............11
  - Hannah's Hopeless Situation (1 Samuel 1:1-18) ....................12
  - The Power of Faith in the Midst of Despair................................12
  - Hannah's Success: Samuel, the Great Prophet................................13
  - The Journey of Faith: Lessons from Hannah's Life........................14

- The Importance of Patience in Faith . . . . . . . . .16
  - The Role of Patience in Abraham and Hannah's Journey . . . . . . . . . . . . . . . . . . . . .17
  - Patience as a Catalyst for Growth. . . . . . . .18
  - Practical Steps to Cultivate Patience in Our Lives . . . . . . . . . . . . . . . . . . . . . . . . . .19
  - The Blessing of Patience. . . . . . . . . . . . . . . .21
- Faith and Trust in Modern Life . . . . . . . . . . . . .21
  - Application to Today's Success . . . . . . . . . .22
  - The Temptation of Self-Reliance. . . . . . . . .23
  - Faith as a Catalyst for Modern Success . . .24
  - The Call to Trust God in Every Aspect of Life . . . . . . . . . . . . . . . . . . . . . . . . . . . . .26

## Chapter 2. Prayer and Communication. . . . . . . . 27

- The Power of Prayer and Connection with God . . . . . . . . . . . . . . . . . . . . . . . . . . . . .27
- Understanding the Essence of Prayer . . . . . . . .29
  - The Nature of Prayer: A Divine Conversation. . . . . . . . . . . . . . . . . . . . . . . .29
  - The Purpose of Prayer: Seeking God's Will . . . . . . . . . . . . . . . . . . . . . . . . . .30
  - The Power of Prayer: Unlocking Divine Possibilities . . . . . . . . . . . . . . . . . . . . . . . . .31

- The Role of the Holy Spirit in Prayer.....32
- The Joy of Connection: Building a Prayer Habit............................32
- The Power of Prayer in Our Lives ............33
  - Prayer as a Source of Strength............33
  - Prayer as a Source of Comfort ..........34
  - Prayer as a Pathway to Peace.............35
  - Prayer as an Expression of Gratitude.....36
  - Prayer as a Catalyst for Change .........36
- Practical Steps to Enhance Your Prayer Life...37
  - Establish a Consistent Prayer Routine....37
  - Create a Prayer Journal .................38
  - Use Scripture in Your Prayers...........39
  - Practice Silence and Listening ..........39
  - Engage in Corporate Prayer ............40
  - Pray with an Attitude of Gratitude.......40
- The Transformative Power of Prayer in Daily Life.................................41
  - Prayer as a Source of Peace.............42
  - Prayer as a Catalyst for Change .........42
  - Prayer as a Tool for Strength............43
  - Prayer as an Expression of Gratitude.....44
  - Prayer as a Guide for Decision-Making ..44
  - Prayer as a Means of Intercession........45

- Cultivating a Lifestyle of Prayer . . . . . . . . . . . . . 46
  - Establishing a Dedicated Prayer Time. . . . 46
  - Creating a Prayerful Environment . . . . . . . 47
  - Engaging in Prayer Journaling . . . . . . . . . . 47
  - Incorporating Scripture into Prayer. . . . . . 48
  - Joining a Community of Prayer . . . . . . . . . 49
  - Practicing Continuous Prayer. . . . . . . . . . . 49
  - Embracing Silence and Listening . . . . . . . . 50
- The Impact of Gratitude on Prayer . . . . . . . . . . 51
  - Expressing Thanks in Prayer. . . . . . . . . . . . 51
  - The Power of a Grateful Heart . . . . . . . . . . 52
  - Gratitude as a Form of Worship . . . . . . . . . 52
  - The Healing Power of Gratitude. . . . . . . . . 53
  - Cultivating a Habit of Gratitude. . . . . . . . . 54
  - The Cycle of Prayer and Gratitude. . . . . . . 55
- The Power of Community in Prayer . . . . . . . . . 55
  - The Strength of Praying Together. . . . . . . . 56
  - The Impact of Shared Testimonies . . . . . . . 56
  - Finding Prayer Partners. . . . . . . . . . . . . . . . 57
  - Joining a Prayer Group or Church Community . . . . . . . . . . . . . . . . . . . . . . . . . 57
  - Embracing the Power of Intercessory Prayer . . . . . . . . . . . . . . . . . . . . . . . . . . . . . . 58

- Prayer as a Key to Success in Life............59
  - Prayer Provides Divine Guidance for Success...............................59
  - Prayer Aligns Our Ambitions with God's Will............................60
  - Prayer Unlocks Favor and Opens Doors..61
  - Prayer Builds Resilience and Perseverance..........................61
  - Prayer Keeps Us Humble in Success.....62
- The Power of Prayer and Communication with God.................................63

## Chapter 3. Integrity and Honesty..............66

- The Pillars of a Strong Life.................66
- Integrity Begins in the Heart...............68
- Integrity in the Small Things...............71
- Integrity in the Workplace.................74
- Integrity in Relationships and Friendships....79
- The Blessings of Living with Integrity........85
- Embracing a Life of Integrity and Honesty....90

## Chapter 4. Hard Work and Diligence...........94

- The Value of Hard Work and Diligence......94
- The Biblical Foundation of Hard Work.......96

- The Rewards of Diligence ................. 98
- Persevering Through Challenges .......... 100
- The Rewards of Hard Work .............. 103
- Embracing a Diligent Spirit .............. 106
- The Fruit of Diligence ................... 109
- Embracing a Life of Diligence ............ 111

## Chapter 5. Patience and Perseverance ........ 115
- The Power of Patience and Perseverance .... 115
- Cultivating Patience in Our Lives .......... 117
- The Power of Perseverance ................ 119
- Embracing the Journey ................... 122
- The Fruit of Patience and Perseverance ..... 125
- Embracing the Journey of Patience and Perseverance ........................... 128

## Chapter 6. Wisdom and Discernment ........ 133
- The Foundation of Wisdom ............... 133
- The Journey of Wisdom .................. 135
- The Pursuit of Wisdom .................. 138
- The Transformative Power of Discernment .. 142
- The Role of Discernment in Relationships ... 144
- Discernment in Daily Life................. 145
- The Synergy of Wisdom and Discernment... 147

**Chapter 7. Gratitude and Contentment........151**
- The Power of Gratitude ....................151
- Contentment in All Circumstances.........153
- Gratitude in Every Season.................156
- Contentment in God's Provision ...........160
- Living a Life of Gratitude and Contentment .164

**Chapter 8. Serving Others ...................167**
- The Example of Jesus – Our Ultimate Servant....................................167
  - Service is Love in Action...............168
  - A Life Changed by Service .............169
- The Heart of a Servant – Shifting Our Perspective..................................170
  - Freedom to Serve ......................171
  - A Shift in Perspective..................171
  - Serving in Every Season................172
- The Example of Christ – Serving as He Served ......................................174
  - Christ's Approach to Service............174
  - The Call to Follow His Example.........175
  - The Power of Sacrifice .................176
- The Blessings of Serving Others............177
- The Joy of Giving .........................178

- Creating Community and Connection . . . . . . 178
  - The Ripple Effect of Service. . . . . . . . . . . . 179
  - Serving with a Grateful Heart. . . . . . . . . . 180
  - Serving as a Reflection of Christ. . . . . . . . 181
  - The Example of Christ's Service . . . . . . . . 181
  - Our Call to Serve Like Christ . . . . . . . . . . 182
  - The Power of Humility in Service. . . . . . . 183
  - Transforming Lives Through Service. . . . 183
- The Rewards of Serving Others . . . . . . . . . . . 185
  - The Principle of Reaping What You Sow. . 185
  - Unexpected Blessings. . . . . . . . . . . . . . . . . 186
  - Heavenly Rewards . . . . . . . . . . . . . . . . . . 187
  - Serving Through Trials . . . . . . . . . . . . . . . 187
- Serving with Humility. . . . . . . . . . . . . . . . . . . 189
- The Heart of a Servant. . . . . . . . . . . . . . . . . . . 189
- Overcoming Pride . . . . . . . . . . . . . . . . . . . . . . 190
- Valuing Others Above Ourselves. . . . . . . . . . 191
- The Lasting Rewards of Serving Others . . . . 192
- Serving With an Eternal Perspective. . . . . . . 193
- A Legacy of Love . . . . . . . . . . . . . . . . . . . . . . . 193
- Finding Fulfillment Through Serving Others . . . . . . . . . . . . . . . . . . . . . . . . . . . . . . . 194

**Chapter 9. Forgiveness and Letting Go . . . . . . . 196**
- Understanding the Weight of Unforgiveness . . 196
- The Transformative Power of Letting Go . . . . 199
- Embracing Forgiveness as a Daily Practice. . . 201
- Forgiving Yourself to Embrace God's Plan . . . 204
- The Power of Forgiveness in Relationships. . . 207
- Releasing the Past to Embrace the Future. . . . 210
- Building Healthy Boundaries . . . . . . . . . . . . . . 214
- Cultivating a Spirit of Forgiveness . . . . . . . . . . 218

**Chapter 10. Embracing Change and Growth . . . 223**
- Understanding Change through a Biblical Lens . . . . . . . . . . . . . . . . . . . . . . . . . . . 224
  - Biblical Examples of Change . . . . . . . . . . . 224
  - The Role of Trust in Change . . . . . . . . . . . 226
  - The Power of Prayer in Navigating Change . . . . . . . . . . . . . . . . . . . . . . . . . . . . 226
  - Embracing a Growth Mindset . . . . . . . . . 227
  - Practicing Gratitude during Change . . . . 228
- Preparing for Change with Faith and Intentionality . . . . . . . . . . . . . . . . . . . . . . . . . 228
  - Identifying Areas of Change . . . . . . . . . . . 229
  - Seeking God's Guidance . . . . . . . . . . . . . . 229
  - Setting Intentional Goals . . . . . . . . . . . . . . 230

- Being a Part of a Supportive Community........................231
- Embracing Flexibility and Adaptability...231
- Taking Action Steps..................232
- Celebrating Small Victories............233

**Chapter 11. The Key to Lasting Success........ 235**
- End with this prayer: A Prayer for Guidance and Strength ..................239

# Introduction

In the book of Joshua, chapter 1 verse 8, we find a powerful directive from God: *"This book of the law shall not depart out of thy mouth, but thou shalt meditate therein day and night, that thou mayest observe to do according to all that is written therein: for then thou shalt make thy way prosperous, and then thou shalt have good success."* (KJV)

What does this verse tell us? God is clearly instructing Joshua that true success comes from meditating on His Word and living according to His principles. It's not just about earthly achievements or material wealth. It's about aligning our lives with God's will and trusting in His guidance.

When we think about success, our minds often jump to the modern definition found in the Merriam-Webster Dictionary: *"Success is the fact of getting or achieving wealth, respect, or fame."* By the world's standards, success often revolves around personal accomplishments, financial gain, or recognition. But the Bible presents a much deeper understanding. Biblical success transcends material wealth or personal accolades. It involves a life lived in alliance with God's plan, and more importantly, in the purpose for which He created each of us.

God-centered success is about more than fame, money, or worldly accolades. It's about thriving in every area of life—whether in our relationships, careers, or personal growth—by prioritizing God's role in everything we do. Without God, no matter how much we achieve, we risk building a fragile foundation that may not withstand the trials and uncertainties of life.

## SUCCESS BEYOND THE SURFACE

When we look at the different aspects of life—career, marriage, business, or even personal well-being—success can have various meanings. But in all these areas, one principle remains constant: without God, there is no true, lasting success. God's presence is the source of strength, wisdom, and the grace needed to thrive.

We see this echoed in Matthew 6:33, which tells us: *"But seek ye first the kingdom of God, and His righteousness, and all these things shall be added unto you."*

This verse is essential because it reveals that success, if pursued outside of God's will, is incomplete. You can achieve the wealth, recognition, or status the world offers, but without God at the center, it lacks substance, direction, and lasting fulfillment. Many people who have chased after fame or riches without God eventually come to regret it. The emptiness they feel is a stark reminder that success apart from God is like a house built on sand—it cannot stand firm when life's storms come.

Take, for example, the warning in Deuteronomy 8:18: *"But thou shalt remember the Lord thy God: for it is He that giveth thee power to get wealth."* This verse touches the truth that all we accomplish and possess ultimately comes from God. He is the source of our strength, talents, and opportunities. Without His blessing and guidance, our efforts amount to little long term.

## BIBLICAL EXAMPLES OF SUCCESS

Throughout the Bible, we see countless examples of individuals who recognized God's role in their success. Abraham, Isaac, Jacob (Israel), and others who leaned on God's wisdom and obeyed His commands experienced not only material success but also the fulfillment of God's promises in their lives. Their success wasn't just in riches but in their obedience to God, their faith, and the legacy they left behind.

For example, Abraham didn't become the father of many nations simply through his own effort or wisdom. It was through his faith in God and willingness to follow Him, even when it meant leaving behind everything familiar. His story teaches us that true success is not about what we can accomplish on our own but about partnering with God and allowing Him to guide our steps.

On the other hand, the Bible also warns us about those who sought success through ungodly means. Gehazi, the servant of Elisha, pursued wealth through dishonesty and greed, leading to his downfall (2 Kings 5:20-27). Lot, Abraham's nephew, chose the lush plains of Sodom and Gomorrah, drawn by its worldly allure, only to face destruction. And then there's the parable of the foolish rich farmer in Luke 12:18, who thought he could secure his future by storing up wealth. But his life was cut short because he placed his trust in material things instead of God.

These examples serve as reminders that while success might look different for each of us, there's one constant—without God at the center, it's ultimately meaningless. Proverbs 3:6 encapsulates this perfectly: *"In all thy ways acknowledge Him, and He shall direct thy paths."*

When we put God first, He guides us, leads us, and ensures that our success is not just temporary or shallow but rooted in eternal purpose.

## A FOUNDATION BUILT ON GOD

So, what does this mean for us today? It means that if we want to experience true success—whether in our work, relationships, or personal endeavors—we must place God at the forefront of our lives. We must seek His guidance, trust in His promises, and remain obedient to His Word. Only then can we experience the kind of success that brings both temporal and eternal rewards.

Making God the foundation of everything we do gives us the assurance of success because He never fails. Whether we look at the lives of people in biblical times or in our modern world, we see a clear truth—true success belongs to God. As seen earlier, the people who acknowledged and followed Him were blessed with prosperity, peace, and fulfillment in ways that transcended mere earthly achievement.

As I mentioned earlier, the concept of success is very broad. Success in one area of life does not necessarily mean success in another. Historically, success in business does not guarantee success in family life. Similarly, excelling in education does not automatically translate into a successful career. Each area of life requires its own effort, wisdom, and guidance. And to achieve complete success, we need God to guide us in all aspects of life. That's why Joshua 1:8, the verse we began with, emphasizes the importance of meditating on God's Word and following His commands—this is the path to comprehensive, lasting success.

## THE UNCERTAINTIES OF LIFE

In this world full of uncertainties, where the future is never fully known, it is impossible to ensure success on our own. Whether it's in investments, relationships, health, or any other area, we simply cannot predict what tomorrow holds. Without God, we lack the foresight and wisdom to make decisions that lead to long-term success.

Take Lot's experience in Genesis 13:10, for example. Lot looked toward Sodom and saw what appeared to be a brighter future, a land full of promise and prosperity. Yet, it all turned out to be an illusion—a mirage. The success he thought he saw evaporated in a short time, and he lost everything. This story serves as a warning: without God, even what seems like a sure path to success can quickly vanish.

Conversely, the Bible is full of examples of kings and leaders who put God first in their lives and, as a result, were blessed with both leadership and success. They understood that to be a leader, to be truly successful in life, they needed God's hand on every aspect of their journey. These examples teach us that no matter what kind of success we seek—whether in leadership, family, or business—God must be our foundation.

## FAMILY SUCCESS: JOSHUA'S EXAMPLE

One of the most striking examples of family success in the Bible is Joshua. As a leader, a man of war, and a person of great responsibility, Joshua was incredibly busy. Yet, his family was a testament to his faithfulness to God. In Joshua 24:15, he boldly declares, *"As for me and my house, we will serve the Lord."* This statement is the secret to Joshua's successful family life. Despite his leadership duties and the battles he fought, he remained steadfast in his commitment to God and his family. As a result, there is no record of any scandal or dysfunction in his household—an accomplishment many of today's families long for.

Joshua's example shows us that building a successful family life requires a foundation built on God. His story demonstrates that even in times of great stress, war, and responsibility, success can be achieved if we prioritize our relationship with God.

## CAN WE BUILD A SUCCESSFUL LIFE WITHOUT GOD?

As we reflect on our modern lives, it's worth asking: can we truly build a successful life without God? The answer is no. It is impossible. Without God, the uncertainties of life can overwhelm us. Without His guidance, we can easily be led astray by the pursuit of material success, fame, or worldly recognition, only to find that these things ultimately leave us unfulfilled and lacking true peace.

Real success—whether in our personal lives, careers, families, or spiritual journeys—comes from placing God first. Just as Joshua declared that he and his household would serve the Lord, we must make that same commitment in our lives. By doing so, we secure not only the kind of success the world recognizes but also the deeper, more meaningful success that only God can give.

## THE PITFALLS OF SUCCESS WITHOUT GOD

Looking at the world today, it becomes evident that many people who claim to have achieved success but do not recognize God as their source eventually encounter great downfall. Whether in government, business, the entertainment industry, or even ministry, we witness many stories of people who once appeared prosperous but ended in shame or despair. Their stories are tragic reminders that without God, success is fleeting and often built on a shaky foundation.

The pressure to maintain a public image of success often becomes too muchas they strive to uphold the appearance that others have created for them, and when the weight of that expectation becomes unbearable, they crumble. Some even resort to drastic measures, like taking their own lives, in an effort to protect an illusion of success. In such cases, it becomes painfully clear that God was not the foundation of their so-called achievements. They may have appeared successful to the world, but their internal lives were devoid of peace, purpose, and true fulfillment.

This stark contrast is a powerful reminder that success without God is not only unsustainable but dangerous. When people build their lives on wealth, fame, or power alone, they are like the foolish man in the parable who built his house on sand. When the storms of life come, their so-called success crumbles, leaving nothing but ruin in its place.

## THE EXAMPLE OF ISAAC'S OBEDIENCE TO GOD

The Bible provides numerous examples of people who found enduring success by making God their foundation. One example is Isaac, who is portrayed as a man who sought God's guidance and trusted in His promises. In Genesis 26:2-3, it states, *"And the Lord appeared unto him, and said, Go not down into Egypt; dwell in the land which I shall tell thee of: Sojourn in this land, and I will bless thee."*

Isaac faced a critical decision in this moment. Like many people today, he could have taken matters into his own hands and followed the path that seemed most logical to him. During the time of famine, Egypt likely appeared to be the best option—a place where resources were plentiful, and opportunities for success seemed more certain. But God had different plans for Isaac. He told him not to go to Egypt but to stay in the land of famine, promising to bless him if he remained obedient.

Isaac's decision to trust in God's direction, even when it seemed counterintuitive, became the key to his success. Despite the famine, God blessed him abundantly, and he prospered in the very place where others were struggling. Genesis 26:12 says, *"Then Isaac sowed in that land, and received in the same year a hundredfold: and the Lord blessed him."* This is a powerful lesson for us today. True success comes not from following the most obvious or popular path but from seeking God's guidance and trusting in His provision.

## WORLDLY SUCCESS VERSUS GOD-GIVEN SUCCESS

The distinction between worldly success and God-given success is clear. Worldly success often comes with compromises and sacrifices of one's values, and it is dependent on external validation. Many people in positions of power, wealth, or fame often have to engage in questionable practices or maintain a false image to keep up appearances. Over time, the weight of these compromises catches up with them, and they are left empty, or worse, they experience public disgrace or personal breakdowns.

God-given success, on the other hand, is built on a solid foundation of faith, trust, and obedience to His Word. It is success that comes with peace of mind, contentment, and the assurance that God is in control.

This kind of success cannot be shaken by circumstances because it is rooted in the unchanging nature of God. As it says in Proverbs 10:22, *"The blessing of the Lord, it maketh rich, and he addeth no sorrow with it."*

God's blessings do not come with strings attached. When He blesses us, there is no need to manipulate situations, fear the opinions of others, or protect a false image. His blessings are pure, and they bring joy and fulfillment without the burdens that often accompany worldly success.

The choice is clear: We can either follow the world's definition of success, which is temporary and often leads to sorrow, or we can follow God's path, which leads to lasting success and blessings that enrich every area of our lives. When we make God first in all we do, we tap into the true key to success—one that is not measured by earthly standards but by the eternal rewards of a life lived in obedience and trust in Him.

## THE FOUNDATION OF TRUE SUCCESS

Let us now reflect on the results of Isaac's obedience, as described in Genesis 26:12-13. *"Then Isaac sowed in that land, and received in the same year an hundredfold:*

and the Lord blessed him. *And the man waxed great, and went forward, and grew until he became very great."* The story of Isaac is a profound example of how obedience to God leads to true success. Isaac followed God's instructions, even though it went against what seemed like the logical choice at the time, and as a result, he was blessed abundantly. His obedience led to exponential growth and greatness.

Now, imagine if Isaac had chosen to disobey God and go to Egypt, believing that the grass was greener there. We can only speculate about the consequences, but based on biblical principles, it is clear that things would not have ended well for him. God's plans may not always align with our human logic, but His ways are higher, and His timing is perfect. When we deviate from His path in search of worldly success, we often find ourselves in failure and regret.

The Bible warns of this in Jeremiah 17:11: *"As the partridge sitteth on eggs, and hatcheth them not; so he that getteth riches, and not by right, shall leave them in the midst of his days, and at his end shall be a fool."* This verse speaks of the fate of those who pursue wealth and success by dishonest or unrighteous means. While they may achieve temporary success, it will not last, and in the end, they will face ruin and shame. This is why it is crucial that we make God the foundation of our pursuits. Without Him, even the most impressive achievements will eventually crumble.

However, it is important to understand that following God does not mean we sit idly by and expect success to fall into our laps. God does not condone laziness or a lack of drive. In fact, He calls us to work diligently and with purpose. But in our pursuit of success, we must ensure that we make Him our number one priority. We must remember that true success is more than just financial gain or worldly recognition—it is about living a life that is aligned with God's will and purpose.

Success in life has many dimensions. It's not just about wealth or fame; it's about our relationships, our character, and our spiritual well-being. Unfortunately, in today's world, the *"get rich quick"* mentality has led many astray. People are chasing after money and success by any means necessary, often neglecting God's principles and guidance in the process.

Many motivational speakers offer captivating ideas that appeal to our desires for quick success and personal fulfillment. While some of their advice may be useful, we must be careful to discern whether or not it aligns with the Word of God. As it says in 2 Timothy 2:19, *"Nevertheless, the foundation of God standeth sure."* His Word is unchanging and eternal, and no amount of worldly wisdom can replace the truth that comes from God.

Proverbs 10:22 reminds us, *"The blessing of the Lord, it maketh rich, and he addeth no sorrow with it."* This verse perfectly encapsulates what true success looks like. It is the kind of success that brings joy, peace, and fulfillment without the accompanying sorrow or regret that often follows worldly success. When we trust in God and follow His path, He blesses us abundantly and with no added sorrow.

Success without God is incomplete. You may gain wealth, fame, or power, but without God, those things will never bring lasting satisfaction. Only God can provide the kind of success that is holistic—touching every area of our lives. Whether it's in our careers, relationships, or personal growth, God is the only one who can give us the peace, joy, and fulfillment that true success brings.

As we move deeper into this book, we will continue to explore how God is the key to every form of success. The stories and principles laid out in Scripture provide timeless wisdom for how we can live a life that is truly successful—one that glorifies God and benefits those around us. When we make God first in our lives, we tap into His abundant blessings and discover the true meaning of success.

# CHAPTER 1

# Faith and Trust

## THE POWER OF FAITH AND TRUST IN GOD

In a world filled with uncertainties, doubts, and challenges, we often find ourselves with the question: *"What does it truly mean to trust God?"* Faith is not just a belief; it is the unwavering assurance in the goodness of God, a confidence that transcends our understanding. Let us always remember the powerful words from Hebrews 11:1: *"Now faith is the substance of things hoped for, the evidence of things not seen."*

Faith is the cornerstone of our spiritual lives. It's the bridge that connects our present circumstances to the glorious future God has prepared for us. When we put our trust in God, we open the door to a life filled with possibilities, miracles, and divine success. Proverbs 16:3 reminds us: *"Commit to the Lord whatever you do, and he will establish your plans."* This is a divine promise! When we align our efforts with God's will, we invite His favor and direction into our lives.

So, why is faith so important? Because it lays the groundwork for everything we hope to achieve. Without faith, we are like ships adrift at sea, tossed and turned by the waves of life. But when we anchor ourselves in God's promises, we can navigate through the storms with confidence. The moment you choose to trust God, you step into a realm where the impossible becomes possible. Your dreams, your goals, your desires—everything you hope for can be realized through the power of faith.

As we go on, we will witness how unwavering faith leads to extraordinary success through the stories of Abraham and Hannah. These biblical figures faced seemingly insurmountable odds, yet their steadfast trust in God transformed their circumstances and brought forth blessings beyond measure. Their journeys remind us that our current struggles do not define our destiny. Instead, it is our faith that propels us toward the bright future God has in store for us.

## THE FOUNDATION OF FAITH

As we go deeper into the foundation of faith, let us remember that faith begins with acknowledging the existence of God as the supreme authority over our lives. Romans 10:17 reminds us, *"So then faith comes by hearing, and hearing by the word of God."* This powerful scripture reveals that faith is not merely an abstract concept; it is rooted in the knowledge of God's Word. The more we immerse ourselves in Scripture, the more our faith grows.

### Understanding God's Sovereignty

To truly trust God, we must first recognize His sovereignty. God is not just a deity we call upon in times of need; He is the Creator of the universe, the One who knows the end from the beginning. When we accept this truth, we can approach Him with confidence, knowing that He holds our future in His hands. The beautiful thing about faith is that it takes the focus off our limitations and places it squarely on God's limitless power.

Imagine standing at the edge of a big ocean. The waves crash against the shore, and the expanse of water seems endless. This is a picture of God's greatness. Just as the ocean is filled with possibilities, so too is our faith. When we acknowledge God's supremacy, we open ourselves to the endless possibilities He offers.

## Faith as a Life Force

Faith is the life force that energizes our souls. It transforms our hopes into reality, bringing substance to our dreams. Just as a plant needs sunlight and water to grow, our faith needs nourishment from God's Word. We nurture our faith through prayer, worship, and the company of fellow believers. As we build our relationship with God, our faith will blossom, enabling us to overcome obstacles and pursue our God-given destinies.

## The Importance of Trust

Trust is the action that follows our faith. While faith is the belief that God can do what He says, trust is the assurance that He will do it. We see this beautifully exemplified in the life of Abraham. God called him to leave his homeland and go into the unknown, promising him a great future. In Genesis 12:1, God instructed Abraham, saying, *"Get thee out of thy country, and from thy kindred, and from thy father's house, unto a land that I will shew thee."*

Imagine the courage it took for Abraham to leave everything familiar behind! He didn't have a detailed map or a timeline; he only had God's promise. Yet, Abraham chose to trust God, believing that the One who called him would provide every step of the way. His faith was not passive; it was active and dynamic, propelling him forward into God's destiny for his life.

## Hebrews 11:6: A Faithful Life Pleases God

The writer of Hebrews emphasizes the importance of faith in Hebrews 11:6: *"But without faith, it is impossible to please Him."* God delights in our faith! When we demonstrate our trust in Him, we honor His character and express our confidence in His goodness. Just as a child trusts a loving parent, we are called to trust our Heavenly Father.

As you reflect on your own journey, consider this: Are there areas in your life where you struggle to trust God? Perhaps you're facing financial difficulties, relationship challenges, or health issues. Remember, faith is not the absence of doubt; it is the choice to believe in God's promises despite our circumstances. When you lean into faith, you invite God to work miracles in your life.

## The Reward of Faithful Trust

As we tune our faith and trust in God, we will begin to see the fruits of our labor. The blessings of trusting God are not merely material; they encompass peace, joy, and fulfillment in every aspect of our lives. When we commit our plans to the Lord, as Proverbs 16:3 assures us, He will establish our paths, guiding us toward success and purpose.

## THE STORY OF ABRAHAM: FAITH AGAINST THE ODDS

Abraham's journey is a powerful testament to the incredible impact of faith and trust in God. As we see his story, we see how a simple act of obedience transformed not just his life but the trajectory of nations. Abraham's faith was an active trust in God's promises, even when the path was unclear.

## The Call to Leave the Comfort Zone (Genesis 12:1)

Imagine waking up one morning to find God calling you to leave everything you know. That was Abraham's reality. In Genesis 12:1, God said to Abraham, *"Get thee out of thy country, and from thy kindred, and from thy father's house, unto a land that I will shew thee."* This was no small task. Abraham had to leave behind his homeland, his family, and his comfort zone, stepping into a future he could not see.

What would you have done in his shoes? Would you have hesitated, worried about what you might lose? Or would you have trusted God wholeheartedly, believing that He had something greater in store for you? Abraham chose the latter. His willingness to step into the unknown demonstrates a profound level of faith. He recognized that God had a purpose for him that extended far beyond his immediate circumstances.

## God's Promises and Abraham's Faith (Genesis 12:2)

God didn't just ask Abraham to leave; He promised him something extraordinary in return. In Genesis 12:2, He said, *"And I will make of thee a great nation, and I will bless thee, and make thy name great; and thou shalt be a blessing."* What a promise! God was not only calling Abraham out of his comfort zone but also into greatness.

Abraham had to trust that God would fulfill His promises, even when the evidence of those promises was nowhere in sight. This is where many of us falter. We often want to see the end result before we take that first step of faith. But God requires us to trust Him before we can witness His hand at work. Abraham's response to God's call was a powerful act of faith. He left everything behind, trusting that God would lead him to a future filled with blessings.

## Abraham's Material Success (Genesis 13:2)

As we look at Genesis 13:2, we see the fruits of Abraham's faithfulness: *"And Abram was very rich in cattle, in silver, and in gold."* God kept His promises! Abraham's trust in God led to material success, but even more importantly, it established him as a man of faith. His riches were a testament to God's favor, which flowed from his unwavering belief in God's plan.

It's important to note that Abraham's wealth wasn't the end goal; rather, it was a byproduct of his faith and obedience. When we put our trust in God, we align ourselves with His purpose, and His blessings naturally follow. God desires to bless us, but we must be willing to step out in faith, just as Abraham did.

## Trusting God with Personal Challenges (Hebrews 11:6)

Abraham's journey wasn't without its challenges. He faced numerous trials and obstacles, including the heartache of waiting for the son God promised him. In Hebrews 11:6, we learn that *"without faith, it is impossible to please Him."* Abraham's faith was put to the test when he and Sarah struggled with barrenness.

Despite their old age and the seeming impossibility of their situation, Abraham and Sarah held on to God's promise. They didn't take matters into their own hands; they waited patiently for God's timing. When we face challenges that seem heavy, it's essential to remember that God is faithful to His Word.

Abraham's faith was a journey of growth, learning to trust God even when the path was unclear. He faced doubt and moments of weakness, but he never wavered in his commitment to God. His faith led to the miraculous birth of Isaac, the son of promise. God turned their impossible situation into a glorious victory, demonstrating that faith can conquer any obstacle.

## The Journey of Faith: Lessons for Our Lives

So, as we reflect on Abraham's incredible journey, we see several lessons we can apply to our own lives. First, faith requires action. Just as Abraham responded to God's call, we too must be willing to step out of our comfort zones. God often asks us to do things that don't make sense in the natural, but that's where the magic happens.

Second, trust in God's promises is crucial. We must hold on to what He has spoken over our lives, even when circumstances suggest otherwise. When we put our faith in God, we can rest assured that He will fulfill His Word.

Finally, patience is a key component of faith. The road to success is rarely straight; it often has twists and turns. Abraham's journey teaches us that waiting on

God is part of the process. His timing is perfect, and when we trust in His plan, we will see His goodness manifest in our lives.

In the face of challenges and uncertainties, let us remember Abraham's faith. His unwavering trust in God led to his success and left a legacy of faith that we can draw strength from today. Just as God was with Abraham, He is with us, guiding us to our promised land. Are you ready to step out in faith and trust God for the incredible things He has in store for you? Your journey of faith awaits!

## HANNAH'S STORY: FAITH IN ADVERSITY

Hannah's story is one of profound heartache, unwavering faith, and the miraculous power of God. Her journey teaches us that even in our darkest moments, when hope seems lost, faith can light the way. Through Hannah's experience, we see the importance of trusting God in the face of adversity and how that trust can lead to unimaginable blessings.

## Hannah's Hopeless Situation (1 Samuel 1:1-18)

Hannah was a woman who experienced deep pain and longing. In 1 Samuel 1:1-2, we learn that she was one of two wives of Elkanah, and while Peninnah, the other wife, bore children, Hannah remained childless. In a culture that valued motherhood above all, Hannah's barrenness was a source of immense sorrow. Year after year, she faced the ridicule of Peninnah, who taunted her mercilessly, adding to her emotional burden.

Can you imagine the heartache she felt? The annual pilgrimage to Shiloh, meant to be a time of worship and joy, became a painful reminder of what she did not have. Yet, it was in this challenging circumstance that Hannah demonstrated an incredible strength of character. Instead of succumbing to despair, she turned to God, pouring out her heart in prayer.

## The Power of Faith in the Midst of Despair

In her moment of desperation, Hannah sought the Lord with fervor. 1 Samuel 1:10 reveals her anguish: *"And she was in bitterness of soul, and prayed unto the Lord, and wept sore."* Hannah's tears were not just a sign of her sorrow; they were an expression of her deep faith. She believed that God could change her situation, and she cried out to Him for help.

As she prayed, Hannah made a vow to the Lord, promising that if He granted her a son, she would dedicate him to God's service for life (1 Samuel 1:11). This vow was not made lightly; it was a demonstration of her faith and trust that God could and would answer her prayer. In that moment, Hannah surrendered her desperation and placed her hope in God's hands.

In the midst of her despair, Hannah's countenance began to change. In 1 Samuel 1:18, we read, *"And her countenance was no more sad."* What a transformation! Faith brought her peace before the fulfillment of her request. It's a powerful reminder that faith is not just about the answers we seek; it's also about the peace we find in God, regardless of our circumstances.

## Hannah's Success: Samuel, the Great Prophet

Hannah's faith did not go unanswered. God heard her cry, and in His perfect timing, she became pregnant and gave birth to a son named Samuel. Samuel grew up to become one of the greatest prophets in Israel's history, anointing kings and leading the nation back to God.

Hannah's journey teaches us that faith is not merely about receiving what we ask for; it's about trusting God's plan for our lives. If Hannah had chosen to take matters into her own hands, she might have ended up with a child born out of desperation rather than divine purpose. But instead, her trust in God led to the miraculous birth of Samuel, a child who fulfilled a significant role in God's redemptive story.

It's essential to recognize that Hannah's victory was not just personal; it had a ripple effect that influenced generations. When we trust God in our challenges, we not only open the door for our breakthroughs, but we also position ourselves to be a blessing to others. Hannah's faith turned her sorrow into joy and her longing into purpose.

## The Journey of Faith: Lessons from Hannah's Life

Hannah's story offers profound lessons for us today. First, we must learn to bring our burdens to God. When faced with challenges, it's easy to retreat into ourselves, to wallow in self-pity. But Hannah shows us the power of bringing our needs to the Lord. In her moment of desperation, she didn't turn to despair; she turned to God.

Second, faith requires vulnerability. Hannah bore her soul before God, expressing her deepest desires and pain. When we allow ourselves to be vulnerable with God, we open the door for His healing and restoration.

Third, patience is crucial in our faith journey. Hannah endured years of heartache, but her unwavering trust in God sustained her through the waiting. In moments of waiting, we can often feel lost and discouraged, but it is in these times that our faith can grow the strongest.

Lastly, we must remember that God's plans for us are good, even when our circumstances suggest otherwise. Hannah's story reminds us that God is working behind the scenes, orchestrating our lives for His glory. When we trust Him, we can rest assured that He is in control.

In the face of your own struggles, remember Hannah's unwavering faith. Like her, you may find yourself in a situation that seems hopeless, but God is always ready to respond to those who seek Him with a sincere heart. Your faith can lead to breakthroughs that not only transform your life but also impact the lives of those around you.

Are you ready to bring your burdens before God? He is waiting to hear your cries, ready to turn your pain into purpose. Thinking about your life, every thread of suffering can lead to a beautiful masterpiece of faith and trust in Him. Your story, like Hannah's, is still being written!

## THE IMPORTANCE OF PATIENCE IN FAITH

As we continue our journey through the stories of faith, we must pause to recognize a crucial component: patience. In our fast-paced world, where instant gratification reigns supreme, the virtue of patience can often feel like a lost art. Yet, as we touch the narratives of Abraham and Hannah, we see that patience is not merely a waiting game; it is an active process that fortifies our faith and deepens our trust in God.

## The Role of Patience in Abraham and Hannah's Journey

Both Abraham and Hannah faced prolonged periods of waiting. Abraham received God's promise of becoming the father of many nations, yet he waited years before he saw that promise fulfilled. God had spoken to him when he was 75 years old, but it wasn't until he was 100 that Isaac, the child of promise, was born (Genesis 21:5). Can you imagine the years of waiting? The moments of doubt? Yet through it all, Abraham chose to hold on to his faith.

Similarly, Hannah endured years of barrenness and the emotional turmoil that accompanied it. Each year at Shiloh, as she witnessed Peninnah's children, her heart ached more profoundly. But instead of giving up, Hannah's faith matured through her waiting. She demonstrated a crucial lesson: patience is an active engagement with God's promises, even when the fulfillment seems distant.

The Bible encourages us in James 1:3-4, saying, *"Knowing this, that the trying of your faith worketh patience. But let patience have her perfect work, that ye may be perfect and entire, wanting nothing."* This scripture reminds us that trials and waiting periods are not in vain. They serve a divine purpose, shaping us into who God has called us to be.

## Patience as a Catalyst for Growth

In our impatience, we often seek quick fixes, desperate to move forward without allowing God to complete His work in us. We may pray for a job, a partner, healing, or financial breakthrough, but when the answers don't come immediately, we grow frustrated. We start to question God's promises and His timing.

However, patience is a catalyst for growth. During times of waiting, we are given the opportunity to develop qualities such as resilience, humility, and deeper trust in God. Just as a seed must be buried in the ground and nurtured before it can break through the surface, so too must our faith be cultivated over time.

Consider Abraham: every year that passed without the birth of Isaac was not a wasted year. Instead, each moment strengthened his resolve and deepened his understanding of God's faithfulness. His journey of patience prepared him for the great challenges that lay ahead, including the test of sacrificing Isaac (Genesis 22). It was in those years of waiting that he learned to trust God's character fully.

Hannah's experience offers similar lessons. As she prayed and waited, she didn't merely endure; she grew. Her prayers became more focused, her faith more fervent. When she finally bore Samuel, it was not just a personal victory; it was a testimony of God's faithfulness that would encourage generations to come.

## Practical Steps to Cultivate Patience in Our Lives

So how can we cultivate patience in our own lives? Here are a few practical steps:

1. **Embrace the Process:** Understand that waiting is part of God's design. He is not idle; He is at work, preparing you for what lies ahead. Embrace this time as an opportunity for growth.
2. **Stay Committed to Prayer:** Like Hannah, pour out your heart to God. Make prayer a constant in your life, not just during

difficult times. As you remain connected to God through prayer, your patience will be fortified.

3. **Reflect on God's Faithfulness:** Keep a journal of answered prayers and moments when God has shown up in your life. Reflecting on His past faithfulness can build your confidence in His future promises.
4. **Surround Yourself with Encouragement**: Engage with a community of believers who can uplift you in your waiting. Share your struggles and triumphs; their encouragement can help sustain you through tough times.
5. **Trust God's Timing:** Remember that God's timing is perfect. What may seem delayed to us is often part of a greater plan. Trust that God knows the best moment for your breakthrough.
6. **Practice Gratitude**: In the midst of waiting, cultivate an attitude of gratitude. Thank God for His promises, His presence, and the work He is doing in your life, even if you can't see it yet.

## The Blessing of Patience

Patience is not simply a waiting game; it is an active demonstration of faith and trust in God. When we learn to wait with hope and expectation, we position ourselves to receive the fullness of God's promises. Just as Abraham and Hannah's stories demonstrate, patience is often the bridge that leads us from promise to fulfillment.

As we conclude this section, remember that waiting is not wasted time. God is using your waiting to prepare you for the blessings He has in store. When you feel weary, hold on to the promise that *"they that wait upon the Lord shall renew their strength"* (Isaiah 40:31). Your faith, combined with patience, can lead to extraordinary outcomes that glorify God and fulfill His purpose in your life.

Trust Him in the waiting. Your breakthrough is coming!

## FAITH AND TRUST IN MODERN LIFE

As we go through the complexities of modern life, we must anchor ourselves in the timeless truths of faith and trust in God. The stories of Abraham and Hannah are not just relics of ancient history; they resonate with us today, guiding us through our own challenges and aspirations. In a world that often prioritizes self-reliance and immediate results, we must learn to align our lives with the divine principles that lead to true success.

## Application to Today's Success

In today's fast-paced society, we are bombarded with messages that promote self-sufficiency. We hear that we can achieve our dreams solely through hard work, determination, and a bit of luck. While diligence and effort are undoubtedly important, they must be coupled with a profound faith in God. As believers, we are called to a higher standard. Our success is not merely about what we can accomplish on our own but about how we can trust God to open doors and create opportunities that we could never have imagined.

Consider the challenges you face in your own life—whether in your career, relationships, or personal growth. Are you relying solely on your understanding, or are you leaning into God's wisdom? Proverbs 3:5-6 reminds us, *"Trust in the Lord with all your heart, and lean not on your own understanding; in all your ways acknowledge Him, and He shall direct your paths."* When we place our faith in God, we open ourselves up to divine guidance that can transform our situations.

Faith does not exempt us from trials; rather, it equips us to face them. Just as Abraham went into the unknown with God's promise as his compass, we too can step boldly into our futures. Every challenge you encounter can be an opportunity to witness God's faithfulness and provision. When you trust Him, you can be assured that He is working all things together for your good (Romans 8:28).

## The Temptation of Self-Reliance

While it's essential to pursue our goals with passion and perseverance, we must be cautious of the temptation to rely solely on ourselves. In our pursuit of success, we may inadvertently neglect our relationship with God, believing that our efforts alone will yield the desired results. This self-reliance can lead to frustration, burnout, and a sense of disconnection from our Creator.

The Bible warns us about this danger in Jeremiah 17:5: *"Cursed is the man who trusts in man and makes flesh his strength, whose heart departs from the Lord."* When we place our trust in our abilities, we risk missing out on the abundant life God has for us. Success achieved without God's guidance can often lead to sorrow, as it lacks the divine blessing that brings true fulfillment.

Let's take a moment to reflect on our own lives. Are there areas where you've been relying on your strength instead of trusting God? It might be in your job, your relationships, or your personal goals. Ask yourself if you've consulted God in your decision-making. Are you willing to surrender your plans to Him, trusting that He has a better way?

## Faith as a Catalyst for Modern Success

Incorporating faith into our daily lives transforms our approach to challenges and opportunities. It encourages us to view setbacks not as failures but as setups for God's glory. Like Abraham, we can navigate the unknowns with courage and confidence, knowing that our faith is our anchor.

Here are a few practical ways to integrate faith and trust into your everyday life:

1. **Daily Devotions:** Start each day with a moment of prayer and reflection. Seek God's guidance in your plans and decisions, inviting Him to direct your path.
2. **Set God-Centered Goals:** As you pursue your aspirations, consider how your goals align with God's purpose for your life. Ask Him to bless your endeavors and provide wisdom along the way.
3. **Surround Yourself with Faith-Builders:** Connect with a community of believers who can encourage and support you. Share your goals and seek prayer from those who understand the power of faith.
4. **Practice Gratitude:** Cultivate an attitude of gratitude, acknowledging God's hand in your successes and His presence in your struggles. Gratitude shifts our focus from what we lack to what we have in Christ.
5. **Be Open to God's Leading:** Stay sensitive to the Holy Spirit's guidance. Be willing to adjust your plans if you sense God leading you in a different direction. Trust that His ways are higher than your ways.

## The Call to Trust God in Every Aspect of Life

As we conclude this chapter, let us remember that faith and trust in God are not just concepts we read about; they are the lifeblood of our existence as believers. When we embrace these principles, we unlock a life of purpose, direction, and abundant blessings.

Faith is not a one-time decision but a continuous journey of reliance on God. Each step of faith is a step toward discovering the fullness of what He has for us. Trust that He knows your heart's desires and is working on your behalf.

As you face the challenges of modern life, remember the stories of Abraham and Hannah. Let their faith inspire you to trust God in every area of your life—business, relationships, health, and personal growth. With God as your foundation, success is not just a possibility; it is a promise. Your faith will lead you to victory, and as you trust Him, you will witness the extraordinary unfolding of His plans in your life.

So step forward with confidence, knowing that your faith and trust in God can shape your destiny and lead you into the abundant life He has prepared for you!

## CHAPTER 2

# Prayer and Communication

### THE POWER OF PRAYER AND CONNECTION WITH GOD

As we journey deeper into our relationship with God, we find ourselves standing at the crossroads of faith and communication. In Chapter 1, we explored the foundation of faith and trust, recognizing that faith is the compass guiding us through life's uncertainties. But faith alone, my friend, is not enough. To fully embrace the promises of God, we must couple our faith with the powerful practice of prayer. Prayer is not just a ritual; it is the lifeline that connects us to our

Heavenly Father, allowing us to commune with Him and experience His presence in our lives.

Philippians 4:6-7 invites us to approach God with our requests, saying, *"Be anxious for nothing, but in everything by prayer and supplication, with thanksgiving, let your requests be made known to God."* This verse reassures us that we are not alone in our struggles; we have a God who is waiting to hear our hearts. When we surrender our anxieties to Him in prayer, something miraculous happens: the peace of God, which surpasses all understanding, guards our hearts and minds.

In the hustle and bustle of our everyday lives, it is easy to lose sight of the power of prayer. However, as we go into this chapter, let us remember 1 Thessalonians 5:16-18, which encourages us to *"Rejoice always, pray without ceasing, in everything give thanks; for this is the will of God in Christ Jesus for you."* Prayer is not just a momentary escape; it is a continuous conversation that enriches our souls and aligns us with God's purpose.

So, as we embark on this journey of prayer, let's recognize that it is a two-way street—a profound dialogue between us and our Creator. Just as faith is the foundation, prayer is the means by which we build and strengthen that relationship. It is through prayer that we find direction in our lives, peace in our hearts, and the courage to face life's challenges.

## UNDERSTANDING THE ESSENCE OF PRAYER

Prayer is often viewed as a simple act—just a few words whispered in the quiet of our hearts. Yet, it is so much more. It is the lifeline that connects us to our Creator, a sacred conversation that nourishes our souls and guides our steps. In this section, we will explore what prayer truly means, its significance in our lives, and how it can be the catalyst for transformation.

### The Nature of Prayer: A Divine Conversation

At its core, prayer is a dialogue with God. It's not merely about presenting our wish lists or voicing our complaints; it's about opening our hearts and minds to a loving Father who desires to commune with us. Just as we engage in conversations with our friends and family, God longs for the same kind of intimacy with us. Prayer allows us to express our thoughts, emotions, and desires, but it also opens the door for God to speak into our lives.

Jesus exemplified this divine conversation during His time on Earth. He often withdrew to lonely places to pray, seeking solitude to connect with His Father. Luke 5:16 tells us, *"But Jesus often withdrew to lonely places and prayed."* This is a powerful reminder that even the Son of God prioritized prayer. If He needed to communicate with the Father, how much more do we? When we approach prayer as a sacred exchange rather than a mere obligation, we begin to unlock its true potential.

## The Purpose of Prayer: Seeking God's Will

Many of us approach prayer with specific requests, hoping to receive what we want. However, prayer's true purpose extends beyond our desires. It is about aligning ourselves with God's will for our lives. As we pray, we invite God into our situations, seeking His guidance and wisdom. This attitude transforms prayer into a tool for discernment and understanding.

James 1:5 encourages us, *"If any of you lacks wisdom, let him ask of God, who gives to all liberally and without reproach, and it will be given to him."* When we seek God in prayer, we are acknowledging that His wisdom far exceeds our own. We become open to His direction, which often leads us to paths we may not have considered.

## The Power of Prayer: Unlocking Divine Possibilities

There is immeasurable power in prayer. It is through prayer that we tap into the limitless resources of heaven. When we pray with faith, we invite God's presence into our circumstances, and that changes everything. Philippians 4:6-7 reminds us that prayer can turn anxiety into peace. When we bring our burdens to God, we are assured that He will replace our worries with His tranquility.

Moreover, prayer fosters an environment where miracles can occur. In Matthew 21:22, Jesus declares, *"And whatever you ask in prayer, you will receive, if you have faith."* This promise encourages us to approach God with boldness, knowing that He is capable of doing the impossible. Our prayers become the channels through which God's power flows into our lives and the lives of others.

## The Role of the Holy Spirit in Prayer

As we navigate our prayer lives, we are not alone. The Holy Spirit serves as our guide, helping us articulate the deepest desires of our hearts. Romans 8:26 assures us, *"Likewise the Spirit helps us in our weakness. For we do not know what to pray for as we ought, but the Spirit himself intercedes for us with groanings too deep for words."* In moments when we feel overwhelmed or uncertain, the Holy Spirit intercedes on our behalf, translating our unspoken yearnings into prayers that reach the heart of God.

When we acknowledge the Holy Spirit's role in our prayer life, we allow ourselves to be led into deeper intimacy with God. We become receptive to His whispers and promptings, which can transform our understanding of prayer from a duty into a delight.

## The Joy of Connection: Building a Prayer Habit

In this fast-paced world, carving out time for prayer can feel daunting. However, it is essential to establish a consistent prayer habit. Start small—set aside a few moments each day to connect with God. Whether it's during your morning coffee or as you wind down at night, creating intentional moments for prayer will deepen your relationship with the Lord.

Consider incorporating various forms of prayer, such as thanksgiving, intercession, and worship. Each approach offers unique benefits, allowing you to experience the fullness of God's presence. Remember, prayer doesn't need to be formal or structured; it can be as simple as talking to a friend. As you cultivate this habit, you will find joy in your connection with God, and it will transform every area of your life.

## THE POWER OF PRAYER IN OUR LIVES

Prayer is not just a routine we follow; it is a powerful weapon in our spiritual arsenal. In this section, we will see how prayer can transform our circumstances, provide comfort in our trials, and cultivate a spirit of gratitude and joy in our daily lives. By understanding the multifaceted power of prayer, we can embrace it as an essential part of our walk with God.

### Prayer as a Source of Strength

Life can be overwhelming, filled with challenges that seem too big. Yet, prayer has the incredible ability to fortify us in our weakest moments. In 2 Corinthians 12:9, Paul shares God's reassuring words: *"My grace is sufficient for you, for my power is made perfect in weakness."* When we bring our struggles to God in prayer, we acknowledge our limitations and invite His strength to fill us.

Consider the story of David in the Psalms. Time and again, he poured out his heart to God, expressing his fears, doubts, and pain. Yet, each time, he found renewed strength and encouragement. In Psalm 34:17-18, he writes, *"The righteous cry out, and the Lord hears them; he delivers them from all their troubles. The Lord is close to the brokenhearted and saves those who are crushed in spirit."* Prayer enables us to cast our burdens on the Lord, allowing His strength to uplift and empower us.

**Prayer as a Source of Comfort**

In moments of grief and sorrow, prayer becomes our sanctuary. When we face loss or disappointment, turning to God in prayer provides solace and healing. Philippians 4:6-7 assures us, *"Do not be anxious about anything, but in every situation, by prayer and petition, with thanksgiving, present your requests to God. And the peace of God, which transcends all understanding, will guard your hearts and your minds in Christ Jesus."*

Through prayer, we can find comfort in knowing that we are not alone. God promises to be with us in our darkest hours, wrapping us in His love and peace. When we reach out to Him, we invite His presence into our pain, and His comfort becomes our refuge.

## Prayer as a Pathway to Peace

As we navigate life's uncertainties, prayer serves as a pathway to peace. When we approach God with our anxieties and fears, He replaces them with a profound sense of calm. Imagine standing on the edge of a stormy sea, with waves crashing all around. In the midst of that chaos, prayer acts as the anchor that steadies our hearts.

In John 14:27, Jesus offers us this promise: *"Peace I leave with you; my peace I give you. I do not give to you as the world gives. Do not let your hearts be troubled and do not be afraid."* When we immerse ourselves in prayer, we allow God's peace to wash over us, calming the storms within and granting us the assurance that He is in control.

## Prayer as an Expression of Gratitude

Prayer is also a powerful way to cultivate gratitude in our lives. It shifts our focus from what we lack to recognizing the abundance God has already provided. When we approach prayer with a heart of thanksgiving, we invite joy and appreciation into our daily lives.

1 Thessalonians 5:16-18 reminds us, *"Rejoice always, pray continually, give thanks in all circumstances; for this is God's will for you in Christ Jesus."* Gratitude transforms our perspective, helping us to see the blessings amidst our challenges. When we take time to thank God in prayer, we acknowledge His goodness and faithfulness, reinforcing our trust in His plans.

## Prayer as a Catalyst for Change

When we pray, we open ourselves up to God's transformative power. Prayer invites divine intervention into our circumstances and situations. We must remember that prayer is not just about changing our circumstances; it is also about changing our hearts. As we pray, we align our desires with God's will, allowing Him to mold us into the people He created us to be.

In James 5:16, we find this profound truth: *"The prayer of a righteous person is powerful and effective."* Our prayers can ignite change in ourselves, our relationships, and our communities. When we intercede for others, we become vessels through which God can work miracles. Prayer has the potential to shift atmospheres, heal brokenness, and restore hope.

## PRACTICAL STEPS TO ENHANCE YOUR PRAYER LIFE

While prayer is a powerful tool in our spiritual journey, it's essential to cultivate a vibrant and meaningful prayer life. In this section, we will go through practical steps that can help you deepen your connection with God through prayer. By incorporating these practices into your daily routine, you will experience a transformation in your spiritual life, allowing prayer to become a source of strength, comfort, and guidance.

### Establish a Consistent Prayer Routine

Just as we prioritize our daily activities, establishing a consistent prayer routine helps us stay connected with God. Setting aside specific times each day for prayer fosters discipline and intentionality in our relationship with Him. Whether it's early in the morning before the world awakens or in the quiet moments of the evening, find a time that works best for you.

Consider the words of Psalm 5:3: *"In the morning, Lord, you hear my voice; in the morning I lay my requests before you and wait expectantly."* Creating a sacred space for prayer invites God into our daily lives, allowing us to begin and end our days with a heart focused on Him.

## Create a Prayer Journal

A prayer journal serves as a tangible record of your conversations with God. Writing down your prayers not only helps you articulate your thoughts and feelings but also allows you to track God's faithfulness over time. You can document specific requests, expressions of gratitude, and revelations you receive during your prayer time.

In Habakkuk 2:2, we are encouraged to *"Write the vision; make it plain on tablets, so he may run who reads it."* As you write in your journal, reflect on God's answers and how He is working in your life. This practice cultivates a deeper awareness of His presence and encourages a posture of gratitude.

## Use Scripture in Your Prayers

Incorporating Scripture into your prayers enriches your communication with God and aligns your heart with His will. As you pray, reflect on verses that resonate with your situation, allowing them to guide your petitions and expressions of praise. The Word of God is alive and powerful, and using it in your prayers invites His truth into your circumstances.

In Matthew 4:4, Jesus reminds us, *"Man shall not live by bread alone, but by every word that comes from the mouth of God."* When we pray Scripture, we declare God's promises and remind ourselves of His faithfulness. This practice not only strengthens our faith but also deepens our understanding of His character.

## Practice Silence and Listening

Prayer is not only about speaking; it is also about listening. In our fast-paced world, it's easy to fill our prayer time with our requests and concerns. However, God desires to communicate with us, and we must make space to hear His voice.

In Psalm 46:10, God says, *"Be still, and know that I am God."* Take moments of silence during your prayer time to quiet your mind and heart, allowing God to speak to you. This practice cultivates a deeper intimacy with Him and enables us to discern His guidance and direction.

## Engage in Corporate Prayer

While personal prayer is vital, engaging in corporate prayer with others strengthens our faith community and allows us to support one another in prayer. Joining a prayer group, attending church prayer meetings, or participating in prayer chains fosters a sense of unity and accountability.

In Matthew 18:20, Jesus assures us, *"For where two or three gather in my name, there am I with them."* Praying with others ignites a powerful synergy, allowing us to witness God move in remarkable ways. Sharing our burdens and praying for one another deepens our relationships and encourages spiritual growth.

## Pray with an Attitude of Gratitude

Gratitude is a powerful force that transforms our prayers from mere requests into heartfelt conversations with God. As you approach Him in prayer, take time to express your thanks for His blessings, provision, and faithfulness.

Philippians 4:6-7 reminds us to present our requests with thanksgiving, and this practice fosters a spirit of joy and contentment. Gratitude shifts our focus from what we lack to recognizing God's abundant goodness in our lives. When we cultivate an attitude of gratitude, we open our hearts to receive more of His blessings.

## THE TRANSFORMATIVE POWER OF PRAYER IN DAILY LIFE

Prayer is not just a ritual or a list of requests; it is a dynamic relationship that transforms our everyday experiences. When we commit to cultivating a robust prayer life, we invite God into our daily routines, allowing His presence to permeate every aspect of our lives. In this section, we will explore how prayer can lead to profound changes in our hearts, minds, and actions, enabling us to navigate life with grace, confidence, and a renewed perspective.

## Prayer as a Source of Peace

In moments of chaos and uncertainty, prayer serves as our refuge. Philippians 4:6-7 reassures us: *"Do not be anxious about anything, but in every situation, by prayer and petition, with thanksgiving, present your requests to God. And the peace of God, which transcends all understanding, will guard your hearts and your minds in Christ Jesus."*

When we bring our worries and fears to God, we exchange our anxiety for His peace. This peace is not contingent upon our circumstances but is rooted in the assurance that God is in control. As we pray, we can release our burdens and trust that He is working all things for our good (Romans 8:28). This transformation brings clarity to our thoughts, steadiness to our hearts, and a calmness that can only come from God.

## Prayer as a Catalyst for Change

Prayer ignites the power of God to bring about change—not only in our situations but also within us. When we earnestly seek God in prayer, we open ourselves to His transformative work. The Holy Spirit begins to shape our hearts, aligning our desires with His will.

James 5:16 reminds us, *"The prayer of a righteous person is powerful and effective."* When we pray with sincerity and faith, we tap into the divine power that can shift mountains, heal hearts, and restore relationships. Our prayers can create ripples of change in our lives, our families, and our communities as we become vessels of His love and grace.

## Prayer as a Tool for Strength

Life's challenges can leave us feeling overwhelmed and defeated. However, prayer empowers us to face our struggles with strength and resilience. In Isaiah 40:31, we find encouragement: *"But those who hope in the Lord will renew their strength. They will soar on wings like eagles; they will run and not grow weary; they will walk and not be faint."*

Through prayer, we receive the strength to endure difficult seasons. When we feel weak, our prayers connect us to God's limitless power, reminding us that we are not alone. In our moments of desperation, we can find solace in knowing that He equips us to rise above our circumstances, turning our trials into triumphs.

## Prayer as an Expression of Gratitude

When we incorporate gratitude into our prayer life, we shift our focus from our needs to God's goodness. Recognizing and thanking Him for His blessings cultivates a heart of gratitude, allowing us to see the beauty in our daily lives. As we express our thanks, we invite joy and contentment to fill our hearts.

Psalm 107:1 encourages us: *"Give thanks to the Lord, for he is good; his love endures forever."* This attitude of gratitude transforms our perspective, enabling us to appreciate the small victories and blessings that often go unnoticed. Prayer becomes an opportunity to celebrate God's faithfulness and to acknowledge His hand in every situation.

## Prayer as a Guide for Decision-Making

In a world filled with choices and uncertainties, prayer is our compass. When faced with decisions, turning to God in prayer allows us to seek His guidance and wisdom. In James 1:5, we are assured, *"If any of you lacks wisdom, you should ask God, who gives generously to all without finding fault, and it will be given to you."*

As we pray for discernment, God reveals His will, helping us navigate life's complexities. By committing our plans to Him, we can trust that He will direct our paths (Proverbs 3:5-6). This connection through prayer empowers us to make decisions rooted in faith rather than fear, leading to outcomes that align with His purpose for our lives.

**Prayer as a Means of Intercession**

Intercessory prayer allows us to stand in the gap for others, bringing their needs before God. As we pray for friends, family, and even strangers, we participate in a divine partnership that can bring healing, hope, and restoration.

Ephesians 6:18 encourages us to *"pray in the Spirit on all occasions with all kinds of prayers and requests."* Our intercession has the power to impact lives and bring about change in ways we may never fully understand. This act of selflessness not only blesses those we pray for but also deepens our relationship with God as we align our hearts with His compassion.

##  CULTIVATING A LIFESTYLE OF PRAYER

As we draw near to God through prayer, we must recognize that cultivating a vibrant prayer life requires intentionality and commitment. It's not merely about setting aside time to pray but about weaving prayer into the very fabric of our daily existence. So, let's quickly see practical steps to develop a lifestyle of prayer that deepens our connection with God and enhances our spiritual growth.

### Establishing a Dedicated Prayer Time

To build a meaningful prayer life, it's essential to establish a dedicated time to communicate with God. Just as we prioritize meetings, appointments, and family time, we must prioritize our time with the Lord. Psalm 55:17 encourages us: *"Evening, morning, and noon I cry out in distress, and he hears my voice."*

Finding a specific time to pray—whether early in the morning, during a lunch break, or before bedtime—sets the stage for consistent communication. This dedicated time becomes a sacred space where we can pour out our hearts, listen for His voice, and experience His presence. As we honor this commitment, we will find that our relationship with God grows deeper and more intimate.

## Creating a Prayerful Environment

Our surroundings can significantly influence our ability to pray effectively. Creating a prayerful environment—whether at home, in our offices, or even outdoors—can enhance our focus and connection with God. This may include setting up a quiet corner with inspiring scriptures, candles, or other items that remind us of God's presence.

Consider the space where you pray. Is it conducive to reflection and connection? Does it invite peace and tranquility? When we create an environment that fosters prayer, we allow ourselves to engage more fully with God, tuning out distractions and opening our hearts to His presence.

## Engaging in Prayer Journaling

Prayer journaling is a powerful practice that enables us to articulate our thoughts, feelings, and prayers in written form. It allows us to document our conversations with God, track answered prayers, and reflect on His faithfulness over time. In Habakkuk 2:2, we are reminded: *"Write down the revelation and make it plain on tablets so that a herald may run with it."*

By keeping a prayer journal, we can capture our hopes, struggles, and experiences in our walk with God. This practice not only helps us stay focused during prayer but also serves as a testament to God's goodness when we revisit our entries and see how He has worked in our lives.

## Incorporating Scripture into Prayer

Integrating scripture into our prayers enriches our conversations with God and aligns our hearts with His Word. When we pray with scripture, we tap into the promises, truths, and wisdom found in the Bible, allowing them to guide our petitions and praises.

For instance, when praying for peace, we might incorporate Philippians 4:6-7, affirming our trust in God's provision. When seeking guidance, we can pray Proverbs 3:5-6, acknowledging our dependence on Him. By praying using scripture, we invite the power of God's Word into our prayers, strengthening our faith and increasing our awareness of His presence.

## Joining a Community of Prayer

Incorporating prayer into our lives can be greatly enriched by connecting with others who share our desire to seek God. Joining a prayer group, church community, or accountability partner can provide support, encouragement, and inspiration in our prayer journeys. Matthew 18:20 tells us: *"For where two or three gather in my name, there am I with them."*

Praying with others fosters a sense of unity and strengthens our faith. Sharing prayer requests and testimonies of God's faithfulness creates a culture of encouragement and accountability. In these spaces, we can grow together in faith, learn from one another, and experience the transformative power of corporate prayer.

## Practicing Continuous Prayer

In 1 Thessalonians 5:16-18, Paul instructs us: *"Rejoice always, pray continually, give thanks in all circumstances; for this is God's will for you in Christ Jesus."* Continuous prayer is not limited to formal moments of prayer; it is about cultivating a mindset of openness to God throughout our day.

We can practice continuous prayer by inviting God into our daily activities—thanking Him for blessings, seeking His guidance in decisions, and lifting up concerns as they arise. This attitude of continual communication transforms mundane moments into sacred encounters with God. By maintaining a posture of prayerfulness, we can experience His presence in every aspect of our lives.

## Embracing Silence and Listening

Prayer is not solely about speaking to God; it is also about listening to Him. In our fast-paced lives, we often fill our prayer time with words, leaving little room for God to speak. Embracing silence and stillness allows us to hear His voice more clearly.

Psalm 46:10 encourages us: *"Be still, and know that I am God."* Taking time to be quiet in His presence opens our hearts to receive guidance, comfort, and clarity. When we listen, we create space for God to speak into our lives, revealing His plans and purposes in ways we may not have anticipated.

## THE IMPACT OF GRATITUDE ON PRAYER

Gratitude is a vital component of a flourishing prayer life. When we approach God with a heart full of thanksgiving, we acknowledge His goodness, faithfulness, and love. This attitude not only enhances our prayers but also shifts our perspective on life, helping us to see the blessings that surround us every day. In this section, we will delve into the powerful connection between gratitude and prayer, exploring how cultivating a thankful heart can transform our communication with God.

### Expressing Thanks in Prayer

One of the most beautiful aspects of prayer is the opportunity to express our gratitude to God. Philippians 4:6 reminds us to present our requests to God with thanksgiving: *"Do not be anxious about anything, but in every situation, by prayer and petition, with thanksgiving, present your requests to God."*

When we include gratitude in our prayers, we acknowledge God's past provision and faithfulness. We honor Him by recognizing how He has worked in our lives, even in the smallest ways. This practice helps to cultivate a heart of contentment, steering us away from feelings of entitlement or dissatisfaction.

## The Power of a Grateful Heart

A grateful heart changes our outlook on life. When we focus on what we are thankful for, we shift our attention from what we lack to what we have. This perspective is transformative and creates a foundation for deeper connection with God.

In Colossians 3:15, we are encouraged to let the peace of Christ rule in our hearts and to be thankful. A grateful heart attracts God's peace, allowing us to approach challenges and uncertainties with confidence and serenity. Instead of worrying about the future, we can rest in the knowledge that God is in control and has our best interests at heart.

## Gratitude as a Form of Worship

Gratitude is not only a response to what God has done; it is also an expression of worship. When we thank God for His goodness, we acknowledge His sovereignty and holiness. This act of worship invites His presence into our lives, enhancing our relationship with Him.

Psalm 100:4 teaches us to enter His gates with thanksgiving and His courts with praise. When we approach God with a spirit of gratitude, we are engaging in worship that honors Him and fosters a deeper intimacy with our Creator. This connection can profoundly influence our prayer life, making our communications with God more meaningful and impactful.

**The Healing Power of Gratitude**

Research has shown that gratitude can lead to significant improvements in mental and emotional well-being. Practicing gratitude reduces stress, anxiety, and depression, fostering a more positive mindset. This healing power extends to our prayer life, enabling us to approach God with a heart full of hope and joy.

In 1 Thessalonians 5:18, we are instructed to give thanks in all circumstances. Embracing gratitude, even during difficult times, helps us to see God at work in our lives, reminding us that His presence is with us, even in the valleys. This perspective allows us to pray with faith and expectation, knowing that God can turn our trials into triumphs.

## Cultivating a Habit of Gratitude

To fully experience the impact of gratitude on our prayer life, we must cultivate it as a daily habit. Here are some practical steps to help us develop this habit:

- **Keep a Gratitude Journal**: Write down three things you are thankful for each day. This practice helps you to focus on the positive aspects of your life and reinforces your awareness of God's blessings.
- **Make Thanksgiving a Priority in Prayer**: Start your prayer time by thanking God for specific blessings before presenting your requests. This sets a tone of gratitude that can transform your entire prayer experience.
- **Share Your Gratitude with Others**: Expressing thanks to those around you—family, friends, coworkers—creates an atmosphere of positivity and encourages others to do the same. Gratitude is contagious!
- **Reflect on God's Goodness**: Take time to meditate on God's promises and His faithfulness in your life. Remembering past blessings can strengthen your faith and inspire gratitude in your current circumstances.

## The Cycle of Prayer and Gratitude

Prayer and gratitude are intertwined in a beautiful cycle. As we pray and present our requests to God, we should also cultivate a heart of gratitude for His past blessings and faithfulness. This cycle deepens our relationship with God and reinforces our trust in Him.

When we approach God with thankfulness, we open our hearts to receive His love and peace. In return, our prayers become more profound, filled with the assurance that He hears us and cares for our needs. This mutual exchange enhances our prayer life, helping us to grow closer to God and experience His presence in powerful ways.

## THE POWER OF COMMUNITY IN PRAYER

In our journey of faith, it's vital to recognize that we are not alone. God has designed us to be in relationship with Him and with one another. The power of community in prayer can amplify our faith and strengthen our connection to God. When we gather together in prayer, we create a space for shared experiences, support, and encouragement, fostering an environment where faith can flourish. These are the benefits of joint prayers:

## The Strength of Praying Together

When believers come together in prayer, there is a unique strength that emerges. Matthew 18:19-20 reminds us, *"Again I say to you, that if two of you agree on earth about anything they ask, it will be done for them by my Father in heaven. For where two or three are gathered in my name, there am I among them."*

There's power in unity. When we pray together, we're not just sharing our individual concerns; we're collectively seeking God's will and inviting His presence into our midst. This communal prayer ignites our faith and creates an atmosphere where miracles can happen.

## The Impact of Shared Testimonies

Sharing testimonies of answered prayers can strengthen our faith and inspire others. When we hear how God has moved in the lives of those around us, it ignites hope and encourages us to persist in our own prayers. Revelations 12:11 tells us, *"And they have conquered him by the blood of the Lamb and by the word of their testimony."*

Each testimony is a declaration of God's faithfulness and a reminder that He is at work in our lives. As we share our stories, we build a community of believers who support one another, celebrating victories and navigating challenges together.

## Finding Prayer Partners

Having a prayer partner can significantly enhance your prayer life. This person can be someone you trust, who shares your values and beliefs. Together, you can pray for one another, hold each other accountable, and celebrate breakthroughs. Ecclesiastes 4:9-10 reminds us that *"Two are better than one, because they have a good reward for their toil. For if they fall, one will lift up his fellow..."*

A prayer partner provides encouragement, support, and a sense of accountability. You'll find that sharing your struggles and joys with someone else deepens your prayer life and fosters growth.

## Joining a Prayer Group or Church Community

Consider becoming part of a prayer group or a church community. This is a powerful way to stay connected with fellow believers who share your desire to grow in faith and prayer. Groups provide opportunities to pray for others, share burdens, and lift one another up in love. As you come together in faith, you will experience the richness of God's presence in a communal setting.

In the words of Psalm 133:1, *"Behold, how good and pleasant it is when brothers dwell in unity!"* This unity in prayer creates an atmosphere of love, support, and encouragement, allowing each person to experience God's grace in tangible ways.

## Embracing the Power of Intercessory Prayer

Intercessory prayer—praying on behalf of others—is a beautiful expression of love and compassion. It's an opportunity to stand in the gap for those who are struggling, lost, or in need of breakthrough. James 5:16 says, *"The prayer of a righteous person has great power as it is working."*

When you intercede for others, you are not only lifting their needs to God, but you are also engaging in a powerful spiritual battle. God honors the prayers of His people, and through intercession, we can make a profound impact in the lives of those around us.

## PRAYER AS A KEY TO SUCCESS IN LIFE

When we talk about success, the world often points to hard work, persistence, and ambition as the ultimate tools. But as believers, we know that true success comes from a deeper place—it comes from being in alignment with God's will, and that alignment is birthed in prayer. Prayer isn't just a religious duty; it is the key that unlocks the door to God's divine plan for our lives, guiding us toward success in every area—our careers, families, health, and personal growth.

These are the benefits of integrating prayer first as a foundation of success:

### Prayer Provides Divine Guidance for Success

One of the most powerful aspects of prayer is the wisdom and direction it brings. Proverbs 3:5-6 reminds us, *"Trust in the Lord with all your heart, and lean not on your own understanding; in all your ways submit to him, and he will make your paths straight."* Prayer helps us step away from our limited understanding and allows us to hear from God, who sees the bigger picture.

When we seek God in prayer before making decisions, we are inviting Him to direct our steps. Whether it's choosing a career path, starting a business, or navigating difficult life choices, prayer positions us to receive God's guidance, leading us to the right opportunities and steering us away from unnecessary struggles. When we follow God's lead, success follows us.

## Prayer Aligns Our Ambitions with God's Will

It's easy to get caught up in the hustle of life and pursue goals that we think will bring fulfillment. But not every ambition leads to lasting success. James 4:3 tells us, *"When you ask, you do not receive, because you ask with wrong motives, that you may spend what you get on your pleasures."* Through prayer, we align our hearts with God's purpose for us.

God's plans for us are always bigger and better than what we can imagine. Jeremiah 29:11 says, *"For I know the plans I have for you, declares the Lord, plans to prosper you and not to harm you, plans to give you a future and a hope."* Prayer helps us surrender our desires and trust that God's plans are greater. As we do so, we find ourselves walking in divine purpose, which leads to true success.

## Prayer Unlocks Favor and Opens Doors

There are moments in life where despite our best efforts, we hit roadblocks. Prayer, however, can unlock supernatural favor and open doors that no man can shut. Philippians 4:6-7 encourages us to *"Be anxious for nothing, but in everything by prayer and supplication, with thanksgiving, let your requests be made known to God. And the peace of God, which surpasses all understanding, will guard your hearts and minds through Christ Jesus."*

When we bring our needs and aspirations to God in prayer, He is faithful to intervene on our behalf. His favor can cause doors to open that seemed impossible to access. Whether it's favor in the workplace, financial breakthrough, or relational restoration, prayer moves the hand of God, aligning our circumstances with His divine provision.

## Prayer Builds Resilience and Perseverance

Success is not always immediate. In fact, it often comes through seasons of waiting, challenges, and perseverance. Prayer is what keeps us strong during those times. As James 1:3-4 reminds us, *"Because you know that the testing of your faith produces perseverance. Let perseverance finish its work so that you may be mature and complete, not lacking anything."*

When we pray, we are refueled with the strength to endure the process that leads to success. Prayer brings us into God's presence, where we receive His peace, comfort, and assurance that He is working all things together for our good (Romans 8:28). It is through prayer that we find the strength to keep going, even when the road is tough.

## Prayer Keeps Us Humble in Success

As we experience success, prayer keeps our hearts anchored in humility and gratitude. Proverbs 22:4 tells us, *"Humility is the fear of the Lord; its wages are riches and honor and life."* When we pray, we acknowledge that all success comes from God, not from our own abilities.

Prayer keeps us focused on the One who blesses us and helps us avoid the pitfalls of pride and self-reliance. As we maintain a spirit of gratitude through prayer, God continues to bless and expand our influence, because He knows we will use our success to glorify Him and bless others.

## THE POWER OF PRAYER AND COMMUNICATION WITH GOD

As we come to the end of this chapter, it's important to take a moment to reflect on the incredible power that prayer and communication with God bring into our lives. We've journeyed through understanding how prayer is not just a religious ritual but a lifeline—a direct connection to the heart of our Heavenly Father.

Prayer isn't just about asking God for things; it's about aligning our hearts with His will, positioning ourselves to receive divine wisdom, and allowing His peace to guard our hearts. Philippians 4:6-7 reminds us that when we pray, *"the peace of God, which surpasses all understanding, will guard your hearts and your minds in Christ Jesus."* It is in that peace that we find strength, clarity, and the courage to pursue our God-given dreams.

Throughout this chapter, we've explored the transformative power of prayer—how it brings us closer to God, fuels our faith, and releases the favor we need to succeed in life. Whether through the examples of Abraham's faith, Hannah's perseverance, or even the promises of God for our own lives, we see a common theme: prayer is the foundation for a life of victory.

We cannot succeed with our own strength. The world might tell us to work harder, try smarter, or rely on self-help solutions. But the Bible teaches us to depend on God in all things. Proverbs 3:5-6 says, *"Trust in the Lord with all your heart and lean not on your own understanding; in all your ways submit to Him, and He will make your paths straight."* It is through prayer that we submit to God, and in return, He directs our steps toward the success He has prepared for us.

Remember, prayer keeps us connected to the source of all wisdom, strength, and provision. It's in those quiet moments with God that we gain the resilience to persevere, the clarity to make wise decisions, and the grace to rise above every obstacle. When we pray, we position ourselves for breakthroughs, miracles, and divine success.

So as you go forward, take with you this powerful truth: the key to unlocking your potential and walking in the fullness of God's promises lies in your relationship with Him through prayer. No matter what you face—whether it's challenges in your career, struggles in your relationships, or desires for personal growth—know that prayer is the bridge between where you are and where God is leading you.

**Keep praying. Keep trusting.** Keep communicating with the One who holds your future in His hands. For it is through prayer that we find not only the success the world sees but the true success of living a life aligned with God's purpose and plan.

As James 5:16 says, *"The earnest prayer of a righteous person has great power and produces wonderful results."* Your prayers have power, and when you stay connected to God, success in every area of your life is not only possible—it's promised.

# CHAPTER 3

# Integrity and Honesty

### ▍ THE PILLARS OF A STRONG LIFE

In life, there are a few principles that stand as the foundation for everything else. They're the anchors that hold us steady when the storms of life come against us. One of those principles is **integrity**. Integrity is more than just being honest—it's living in alignment with the truth in every part of your life. It's about being the same person in public that you are in private. When you walk in integrity, you don't have to worry about being found out, because you're already walking securely in who God created you to be.

The Bible says in Proverbs 10:9, *"Whoever walks in integrity walks securely, but whoever takes crooked paths will be found out."* When you live a life of honesty and integrity, you don't have to hide or worry about what's around the corner. God promises that the righteous will walk in security, but those who compromise or take shortcuts, will eventually stumble.

We've already talked about the importance of faith, prayer, and trusting God with every area of our lives. Now, we're going to build on that by talking about what it means to live with integrity. You see, faith and prayer give us the strength to stand firm, but integrity gives us the roadmap to walk in righteousness. It keeps us aligned with God's truth, even when the world pressures us to cut corners or bend the truth for personal gain.

Integrity isn't just a nice idea; it's the backbone of our success. A person without integrity may rise for a moment, but that success won't last. It's like building a house on sand—sooner or later, it will come crashing down. But a person who walks in honesty and integrity is building their life on a firm foundation. That's the life God can bless.

In every area—whether it's in our relationships, in business, or in the way we handle the smallest of tasks—God is looking for integrity. And when we commit to living by His principles, He'll lead us down paths of blessing and favor.

The truth is, God has set before us a life of abundance, but it's up to us to walk in integrity so we can receive the fullness of His promises. When we walk in integrity, we're not just doing it for ourselves; we're doing it for the generations to come. We're setting a standard for our families, our communities, and for those watching our lives. It's more than what we say; it's about how we live.

So, as we go deeper into this chapter, I want to encourage you to open your heart to what God has to say about integrity. He's calling you to a higher level, a deeper walk with Him and when you commit to living in integrity, you'll discover that God's favor and blessings are waiting on the other side.

## INTEGRITY BEGINS IN THE HEART

Integrity doesn't start with what we do; it starts with who we are. It's not just about our actions—it's about our heart. If we want to live lives of integrity, we first have to allow God to shape our inner world. The Bible tells us in Proverbs 4:23, *"Above all else, guard your heart, for everything you do flows from it."*

If we let dishonesty, greed, or selfishness take root in our hearts, it's only a matter of time before it shows up in our actions. Integrity begins when we allow God to renew our hearts and align our desires with His will. That's why it's so important to stay connected with God, to spend time in prayer, and to fill our minds with His Word. The more we do that, the more our hearts become reflections of His truth.

Jesus said in Matthew 12:34, *"For out of the abundance of the heart the mouth speaks."* In other words, whatever is in your heart will eventually show up in your words and actions. If integrity is planted deep in your heart, you'll naturally live it out. It won't be something you have to force—it will flow from who you are.

That's why living with integrity isn't about perfection. It's about consistently choosing God's way over the world's way, even when no one is looking. It's about making the hard decision to be truthful when it would be easier to lie. It's about choosing honesty in your business dealings, even when it costs you something. It's about standing firm in your values when the crowd is heading in the opposite direction.

Ephesians 4:25 says, *"Therefore each of you must put off falsehood and speak truthfully to your neighbor, for we are all members of one body."* God calls us to put away dishonesty and live in the light of truth. Why? Because integrity isn't just about how we interact with God—it's also about how we interact with others. When we walk in integrity, we build trust, we strengthen our relationships, and we create environments where God's peace and favor can flow.

But it all starts with the heart. If you want to live a life of integrity, begin by examining what's going on inside. Ask yourself: Am I allowing fear, pride, or insecurity to drive my decisions? Am I cutting corners because I'm afraid I won't succeed otherwise? Or am I trusting God to guide me, knowing that His way is always better than the world's shortcuts?

God is more interested in the condition of your heart than in how perfect your actions appear to be. He knows that if your heart is right, your actions will follow. So, before you try to fix anything outwardly, go inward. Let God work on the deep things. Surrender the hidden areas of your life to Him, and watch how He transforms your integrity from the inside out.

Living with integrity may not always be the easiest path, but it's the one that leads to true success—the kind that honors God and blesses those around you. And remember, you don't have to do it alone. God's Spirit is with you, guiding you, giving you the strength to walk in His truth every day.

## INTEGRITY IN THE SMALL THINGS

Integrity isn't just about the big, noticeable moments in life. It's about the small, everyday decisions that shape who we are and how we live. So often, we think of integrity as something we need only when we're faced with a major challenge or a public situation. But in reality, integrity is built in the quiet moments when no one is watching. It's those little choices we make day by day that determine the strength of our character.

Jesus said in Luke 16:10, *"Whoever can be trusted with very little can also be trusted with much."* What this means is that our faithfulness in the small things is a reflection of how we'll handle the big things. If you're honest in the small matters—when the stakes are low and no one's paying attention—God can trust you with more. But if you compromise your integrity when no one's looking, it won't be long before that compromise shows up in larger areas of your life.

Sometimes, we think that cutting corners on the small stuff doesn't really matter. We tell ourselves, "It's just a little thing—nobody will notice." But here's the truth: **God** notices. God is paying attention to those small decisions because He knows they reveal the true condition of our hearts. When you choose integrity in the small things, you're proving to God—and to yourself—that you can be trusted with bigger responsibilities and blessings.

Imagine this: You're at work, and a situation comes up where you could easily take credit for something you didn't do. No one would know. It seems harmless. But in that moment, you have a choice: Will you take the shortcut for personal gain, or will you choose integrity, even if no one else sees it?

Or maybe it's something as simple as returning a little extra change when the cashier gives you too much. It's not a big deal, right? But your decision in that moment reveals whether you value honesty and integrity, even when it doesn't seem to matter much.

Those small decisions may seem insignificant, but they're like bricks in the foundation of your character. Each time you choose integrity, you're building a life that honors God, and you're positioning yourself for greater blessings. But when you compromise, even in the small things, you weaken the foundation. And over time, those little cracks can cause bigger problems down the road.

Proverbs 10:9 says, *"Whoever walks in integrity walks securely, but whoever takes crooked paths will be found out."* When you live with integrity, you don't have to worry about being "found out." You can walk with confidence, knowing that your life is built on the solid foundation of truth and honesty. But when you take shortcuts, eventually, the cracks will show. What you thought was hidden will come to light.

Let me encourage you today: Don't underestimate the power of integrity in the small things. Be faithful in the little areas of your life, and trust that God sees your obedience. He's watching how you handle the small opportunities, and He's preparing you for the bigger ones. Every time you choose integrity, you're sowing seeds that will bring a harvest of blessings in your future.

You may not see the immediate payoff for doing the right thing when no one is watching. But I promise you this: God sees it, and He will reward your faithfulness. He's looking for people who will be faithful in the small things so He can entrust them with more. So be that person. Be the one who chooses integrity, even when it's not convenient, even when it doesn't seem to matter. Because to God, it always matters.

And remember, walking in integrity is a journey. It's not about being perfect all the time. It's about consistently choosing God's way over the world's shortcuts, day by day, moment by moment. When you make integrity a habit in the small things, you'll see how it transforms your life in the big things, too. And God will honor you for it.

## INTEGRITY IN THE WORKPLACE

Just like integrity plays an important role in our personal relationships, it is equally essential in our professional lives. Our workplaces are environments where our character is tested daily. Whether we are employees, business owners, or leaders, how we conduct ourselves in the workplace speaks volumes about who we are and what we value. Integrity in the workplace isn't just about doing the right thing when people are watching—it's about upholding honesty and truthfulness when no one else may notice.

Proverbs 10:9 tells us again, *"Whoever walks in integrity walks securely, but whoever takes crooked paths will be found out."* This scripture reminds us that walking with integrity ensures a foundation of security in all aspects of life, including the workplace. When you operate with integrity, you don't have to worry about being "found out." You can walk confidently because your actions are above reproach.

Integrity in the workplace starts with doing your best. Colossians 3:23 says, *"Whatever you do, work at it with all your heart, as working for the Lord, not for human masters."* This is key: when we approach our work as if we are doing it for God, our mindset shifts. We no longer work just to impress a boss or secure a promotion; we work with excellence because we want to honor God. And when you honor God in your work, He'll take care of everything else.

One of the greatest tests of integrity in the workplace comes when shortcuts are offered. Maybe you've been in a position where cutting corners or being dishonest could have given you an advantage. In those moments, your integrity is being tested. Are you willing to sacrifice long-term success for short-term gain? The enemy loves to present us with opportunities to take the easy way out, but Proverbs 16:8 says, *"Better is a little with righteousness than great revenues without justice."* It's better to do the right thing and earn less than to prosper dishonestly. The truth is, the rewards of integrity may not always be immediate, but they are lasting.

Let's look at the story of Daniel. He was a man of great integrity in his workplace. Daniel served in a foreign government, yet he never compromised his values. Even when those around him plotted against him, trying to find fault with his work, they couldn't because Daniel was a man of integrity. Daniel 6:4 tells us, *"They could find no corruption in him, because he was trustworthy and neither corrupt nor negligent."* His integrity led to God's favor, and ultimately, it allowed Daniel to rise to positions of great influence.

But integrity in the workplace goes beyond our personal actions—it also involves how we treat others. Ephesians 4:25 reminds us to *"speak the truth with your neighbor."* Whether it's a coworker, a client, or a subordinate, our words and actions must reflect honesty and truthfulness. Have you ever faced a situation where telling the truth might have been costly? Maybe it could have caused tension or even put your job at risk. But that's where integrity is truly tested—when telling the truth is hard, but you choose to do it anyway because it honors God and aligns with His principles.

Another aspect of workplace integrity is how we handle responsibility. Are you someone who can be trusted with tasks, big or small? Are you consistent in your work, reliable in your commitments, and honest in your dealings? Luke 16:10 says, *"Whoever can be trusted with very little can also be trusted with much, and whoever is dishonest with very little will also be dishonest with much."* Integrity in the workplace means being faithful with what you've been given, no matter the size of the responsibility. When you're faithful in the small things, God can trust you with greater opportunities.

Think about Joseph again, this time in the context of his work. He was entrusted with the household of Potiphar, and because of his integrity, Potiphar placed everything he owned under Joseph's care. Even when faced with temptation from Potiphar's wife, Joseph remained steadfast in his integrity. He said in Genesis 39:9, *"How then could I do such a wicked thing and sin against God?"* Joseph understood that integrity in his work wasn't just about pleasing his earthly master—it was about honoring God.

And what happened as a result? Even after being falsely accused and imprisoned, Joseph's integrity led him to greater success. He went from being a servant in Potiphar's house to ruling over Egypt. This reminds us that integrity in the workplace may not always bring immediate rewards, but God sees your faithfulness, and He knows how to elevate you at the right time.

Integrity in the workplace also applies to leadership. If you're in a position of authority, your integrity sets the tone for those around you. People are watching how you lead. Are you fair? Are you transparent? Do you keep your word? Proverbs 11:3 says, *"The integrity of the upright guides them, but the unfaithful are destroyed by their duplicity."* A leader who walks in integrity inspires trust and loyalty, while one who is dishonest or deceitful creates an atmosphere of mistrust and division. As leaders, we are called to lead by example, showing integrity in all our dealings.

Therefore, integrity in the workplace is about being true to who you are in every aspect of your professional life. Whether you're making decisions behind closed doors, dealing with colleagues, or handling responsibilities, your integrity matters. It reflects not just on you but on the God you serve. Remember, the reward for integrity may not always be immediate, but it is certain. God sees your heart, and when you walk in integrity, He will bless the work of your hands and open doors no one can shut. Keep walking in integrity, and watch how God uses your faithfulness to bring about success and favor in your professional life.

## INTEGRITY IN RELATIONSHIPS AND FRIENDSHIPS

When we talk about integrity, it's important to remember that it applies not only to our personal conduct and professional lives, but also to our relationships. Relationships—whether romantic, familial, or friendships—are built on trust, and the foundation of trust is integrity. Integrity in relationships means being honest, transparent, and faithful. It means being a person of your word, standing up for what's right, and treating others with kindness, respect, and truthfulness.

Proverbs 11:3 teaches us, *"The integrity of the upright guides them, but the unfaithful are destroyed by their duplicity."* In relationships, nothing can be more damaging than duplicity—pretending to be something you're not or hiding the truth to manipulate situations. Have you ever been in a relationship where someone wasn't completely honest with you? Perhaps it was a friend who promised loyalty but spoke behind your back, or a partner who wasn't truthful about their intentions. When integrity is lacking, trust is broken, and the relationship begins to erode.

Integrity in relationships means showing up as your true self and letting your yes be yes, and your no be no, as it says in Matthew 5:37. People who love and care for you deserve your honesty, even when the truth is difficult to share. Sometimes, we might feel tempted to avoid difficult conversations, sweep things under the rug, or even tell a little white lie to keep the peace. But peace built on dishonesty is fragile and temporary.

In contrast, relationships founded on honesty and integrity can weather any storm because there is a solid foundation of trust.

This is where Ephesians 4:25 comes into play: *"Therefore each of you must put off falsehood and speak truthfully to your neighbor, for we are all members of one body."* In our closest relationships, falsehoods—even small ones—create division. Speaking truth, however, unites us and strengthens our bonds. Whether it's a hard truth or a confession of mistakes, integrity requires that we be truthful because true connection can only flourish in an atmosphere of honesty.

Let's take a look at the example of David and Jonathan in the Bible. Their friendship is one of the most beautiful examples of integrity and loyalty in Scripture. Jonathan was the son of King Saul, who viewed David as a threat to his throne. Jonathan, though, loved David as his own soul, and despite his father's hatred toward David, Jonathan remained loyal and honest in his relationship with him. 1 Samuel 20:17 shows the depth of their bond, saying, *"Jonathan made David reaffirm his oath out of love for him, because he loved him as he loved himself."*

This kind of integrity in friendships—where there is loyalty, honesty, and selflessness—is a gift from God. It's not easy to find friends who stand by you in all seasons, but integrity allows those friendships to thrive. If you're blessed with friends like Jonathan, cherish them, and honor them with integrity. If you haven't yet found those relationships, remember that as you walk in integrity, God will bring the right people into your life.

Integrity in romantic relationships is also crucial. Whether you're dating or married, honesty and faithfulness are the bedrock of a strong relationship. Colossians 3:9 says, *"Do not lie to each other, since you have taken off your old self with its practices."* Lying, infidelity, and deception have no place in a relationship that seeks to honor God. The truth may be difficult to speak at times, but withholding it only damages the bond between partners.

In marriage, integrity is expressed through faithfulness—physically, emotionally, and spiritually. Ephesians 5:25 tells husbands to *"love your wives, just as Christ loved the church and gave himself up for her."* And similarly, wives are called to honor and respect their husbands. When both partners walk in integrity, their marriage becomes a reflection of Christ's love for the church—unwavering, sacrificial, and truthful.

But integrity in relationships goes beyond just avoiding lies or infidelity. It also involves living with consistency. If you are one person in public and another in private, it undermines the trust in your relationships. Are you showing the same character behind closed doors as you do in front of others? True integrity means you are the same person no matter who is watching, and that consistency builds trust over time.

Integrity in relationships also means setting healthy boundaries. Sometimes, the most honest thing we can do in a relationship is to say no. Perhaps you've experienced a situation where someone was pushing you to do something that didn't align with your values or asking for more than you could give. Setting boundaries doesn't mean you love or care for someone any less—it means you are protecting the relationship and honoring your own integrity in the process.

In friendships, it's vital to remember Proverbs 27:17, "*As iron sharpens iron, so one person sharpens another.*" True friends hold each other accountable and encourage one another to live with integrity. Do you have friends who sharpen you, who push you to be the best version of yourself, and who challenge you to walk in righteousness? If not, it might be time to reevaluate the people you surround yourself with. God calls us to relationships that build us up and strengthen our walk with Him.

In your relationships, strive to be the kind of friend, partner, or family member who operates with honesty and consistency. When you do, you will attract people with similar values and build relationships that last. As Jesus says in Matthew 7:16, *"By their fruit you will recognize them."* The fruit of integrity in your relationships is deep connection, mutual respect, and lasting trust.

So, whether you are in a marriage, a friendship, or building new relationships, remember that integrity is key. It's what allows love to flourish, trust to grow, and relationships to stand strong even in difficult times. Walking in integrity isn't always easy, but it is always worth it.

## THE BLESSINGS OF LIVING WITH INTEGRITY

As we delve deeper into the subject of integrity, it's vital to recognize the immense blessings that come from living a life rooted in honesty and truthfulness. Integrity isn't just a moral compass; it's the very pathway to a fulfilling and blessed life. The Scriptures remind us in Proverbs 2:7, *"He holds success in store for the upright, he is a shield to those whose walk is blameless."* This is a powerful promise! God Himself is our shield, protecting us as we navigate life's journey with integrity.

When we choose to live with integrity, we align ourselves with God's principles. This alignment opens the door to divine favor and blessings. It's not merely about avoiding wrongdoing; it's about stepping into a life of purpose, where our actions reflect our commitment to God and His Word. Integrity paves the way for genuine success—success that transcends material gains and touches the very core of our being.

Imagine waking up each day with a clear conscience, knowing that your words and actions reflect your true self. Living with integrity gives us a sense of peace that cannot be bought or traded. It's a peace that comes from the assurance that we are living according to God's design, free from the burdens of deception or regret. In this sense, integrity is not just about personal morals; it's a lifestyle that brings us closer to God and deeper into His plans for our lives.

Consider the story of Joseph in the Bible. Joseph was a young man who faced numerous challenges and injustices, from being sold into slavery by his own brothers to being falsely accused and imprisoned. Yet throughout all these trials, Joseph maintained his integrity. He refused to succumb to temptation when Potiphar's wife attempted to seduce him. Instead of compromising his principles for immediate pleasure, he stood firm, knowing that his integrity was worth more than any fleeting desire.

What was the result of Joseph's integrity? Ultimately, God elevated him from the prison to the palace, where he became a ruler in Egypt. Genesis 41:46 says, *"Joseph was thirty years old when he entered the service of Pharaoh king of Egypt."* His integrity brought him not only personal restoration but also the ability to save countless lives during a time of famine. God used

Joseph's unwavering commitment to integrity to fulfill His greater plan.

When we commit to living with integrity, we may not always see immediate rewards, but rest assured that God is at work behind the scenes. His blessings may manifest in various forms—promotions at work, strengthened relationships, and even divine opportunities that seem to come out of nowhere. Integrity positions us to receive these blessings because we are walking in alignment with God's will.

Likewise, when we choose dishonesty or compromise our values, we place ourselves outside of God's protection. Proverbs 10:9 reminds us, *"Whoever walks in integrity walks securely, but whoever takes crooked paths will be found out."* Dishonesty may offer temporary gains, but it ultimately leads to destruction. The truth has a way of surfacing, and when it does, it can shatter our lives and relationships. It is far better to endure short-term discomfort than to face the long-term consequences of a lack of integrity.

Moreover, living with integrity impacts those around us. Our choices serve as a powerful testimony to others. When friends, family, and colleagues witness our unwavering commitment to honesty, it inspires them to reflect on their own choices. They may even ask themselves, **"What is it about this person that allows them to be so steadfast in their integrity?"** Our integrity shines as a light in a world that often promotes deception and dishonesty.

As you go about your daily life, consider how your actions and decisions reflect your commitment to integrity. Are you setting an example for others to follow? Are you being a beacon of truth in your workplace, community, and relationships? Remember that integrity is contagious. When we walk in honesty and truth, we encourage others to do the same.

Let us also not forget that integrity is a reflection of our relationship with God. As we cultivate our walk with Him, our character will naturally align with His. When we are filled with the Spirit, we bear the fruit of integrity. This is why it's essential to maintain our spiritual connection through prayer, as discussed in Chapter 2. Our prayer life fortifies our commitment to integrity, helping us resist temptation and stand firm in our convictions.

Now, let us embrace the call to live with integrity. Let us remember the blessings that flow from our commitment to honesty and truthfulness. When we choose integrity, we are choosing a path of righteousness that leads to lasting peace, fulfillment, and divine favor. We are declaring to ourselves and the world that our lives are grounded in something greater than ourselves—a commitment to God and His principles.

As you reflect on the integrity of your own life, ask yourself: What steps can I take to integrate integrity in every area of my life? How can I strengthen my relationships and be a model of truthfulness for others?

God is with you, and as you walk in integrity, you can trust that He will guide you, protect you, and bless you abundantly. You are not alone on this journey. Together, we can strive for integrity in all we do, reflecting the light of Christ in a world that desperately needs it.

## EMBRACING A LIFE OF INTEGRITY AND HONESTY

As we come to the conclusion of this chapter, let us take a moment to reflect on the profound truth that integrity and honesty are not mere choices but rather the very essence of a life well-lived. When we embrace integrity, we invite God's blessings into our lives, allowing His favor to flow through us and touch every aspect of our being.

In a world filled with shifting morals and fleeting truths, the call to live with integrity stands firm as a beacon of hope. Proverbs 10:9 tells us, *"Whoever walks in integrity walks securely."* This is not just a promise; it is an assurance from God that when we commit to living honestly, we are sheltered under His divine protection. We do not have to fear the consequences of our actions because our hearts are aligned with His will.

So, take into account the legacy of integrity you are building. Your life is a story, and with each choice you make, you write another chapter. The question is, what will your story say? Will it echo the values of honesty and truth, or will it be a tale of deceit and compromise?

Integrity impacts not only our lives but also the lives of those around us. As we model honesty, we inspire others to rise to that standard. Your integrity can be the catalyst for change in your workplace, family, and community. When people see you standing firm in your principles, it ignites a spark within them to do the same. This ripple effect of integrity can transform entire communities, bringing about a culture of honesty and trust.

Let us also remember the divine promise found in Ephesians 4:25, where we are urged to speak the truth in love. Integrity is not just about being honest with ourselves and others; it's about doing so with grace and compassion. As we navigate the complexities of life, may our words and actions reflect the heart of Christ, who embodied perfect integrity.

As you move forward, I encourage you to take practical steps to cultivate integrity in your life. Start by evaluating your daily interactions. Are there areas where you can be more truthful? Are there relationships that need healing through honesty? Make a commitment to yourself and to God to uphold integrity in every situation, no matter how big or small.

Remember that integrity is a journey, not a destination. It requires intentionality and dedication. As we align our hearts with God's principles and seek to honor Him through our choices, we find the strength to resist temptation and the courage to speak the truth, even when it is difficult.

Let us pray for the grace to live lives of integrity and honesty. May we be filled with the Spirit of God, empowering us to uphold truth in a world that desperately needs it. As we walk this path, we can be assured that God is with us, guiding us, and blessing us abundantly.

As we step into the next chapter of our lives, let us carry with us the lessons learned about integrity and honesty. May our lives be a reflection of Christ's light, illuminating the way for others. Together, let us choose to walk securely, knowing that our commitment to integrity not only honors God but also opens the doors to His greatest blessings.

Thank you for embarking on this journey of integrity with me. I look forward to exploring the next powerful principle together as we continue to grow in faith, trust, and the transformative power of living a life dedicated to God. Remember, with each step you take in integrity, you are making a profound impact—not just in your life, but in the lives of those around you. Let's go forth, shining brightly in a world that needs the truth now more than ever.

# CHAPTER 4

# Hard Work and Diligence

## THE VALUE OF HARD WORK AND DILIGENCE

Sometimes, we often encounter the foundational principles that guide us toward success and fulfillment. In our previous chapters, we've explored the importance of faith, trust, and integrity—each a pillar that supports the structure of our lives. Now, we will go into a crucial aspect that ties these principles together: **hard work and diligence**.

God has called each of us to a purpose, and while it's true that faith moves mountains and integrity builds relationships, it's **hard work** that lays the path to our promised land. The Scriptures remind us in Proverbs 14:23, *"In all labor there is profit, but mere talk leads only to poverty."* This powerful verse paints a vivid picture: action is necessary. Hard work is not just a recommendation; it's a requirement for success!

When we look at the world around us, we see countless examples of individuals who have achieved greatness through relentless effort and unwavering diligence. They understood that while faith is vital, it must be coupled with a commitment to roll up our sleeves and get to work. The Bible is full of stories that exemplify this principle, encouraging us to embrace hard work as an integral part of our walk with God.

We can find further motivation in Colossians 3:23-24, which instructs us, *"Whatever you do, work heartily, as for the Lord and not for men."* Imagine the impact on our lives if we approached every task—big or small—as an act of worship! Every moment spent diligently working is a chance to glorify God and reflect His character to those around us.

As we get into the exploration of hard work and diligence, let's commit to embracing the journey. Let's open our hearts to understand that diligence is not just about grinding away at our tasks; it's about aligning our efforts with God's purpose for our lives. It's about honoring Him in all we do. So, let's dig deep, draw inspiration from the Word, and discover how hard work can lead us to the abundant life God promises.

## THE BIBLICAL FOUNDATION OF HARD WORK

To understand the true essence of hard work, we must first look at its biblical foundation. God Himself is a model of diligence. From the very beginning, in the Book of Genesis, we see that after creating the heavens and the earth, He dedicated six days to His work and rested on the seventh. This beautiful example teaches us that work is not just a means to an end; it's part of our divine calling. We were created in His image, and that includes the capacity for hard work and creativity.

In Proverbs 22:29, we read, *"Do you see a man skillful in his work? He will stand before kings; he will not stand before mean men."* This verse highlights that diligence is a pathway to greatness. Skill and excellence in our work open doors of opportunity, and God promises that those who labor faithfully will be rewarded. When we commit ourselves to our tasks, we set ourselves apart.

Moreover, we are reminded in Ecclesiastes 9:10, *"Whatever your hand finds to do, do it with all your might…"* This is not just a suggestion; it's an imperative! When we pour our heart and soul into our work, we not only honor God but also cultivate the skills and talents He has given us. Every effort, no matter how small, contributes to a larger purpose.

Think about it—when you put your best foot forward in your work, you're sowing seeds for your future. Diligence in our daily tasks is what builds a strong foundation for our dreams and aspirations. Remember that every achievement begins with a step. Each day is a chance to invest in your future through hard work, and God sees every bit of it.

It's essential to recognize that hard work isn't always glamorous. There will be days filled with challenges, setbacks, and obstacles. However, this is where our faith comes in. As we rely on God and His promises, we gain the strength to push through adversity. We remember that our labor is not in vain; it is a part of a divine plan.

## THE REWARDS OF DILIGENCE

As we reflect on the importance of hard work, let us not overlook the incredible rewards that come with diligence. The Bible is filled with promises that encourage us to persevere in our efforts. In Proverbs 14:23, we find a powerful truth: *"In all labor there is profit, but mere talk leads only to poverty."* This scripture reminds us that action is essential; it's through our hard work that we unlock the blessings and abundance God has in store for us.

When we commit ourselves to our tasks, we are actively participating in the divine economy of God's kingdom. Each act of diligence is like a seed planted in fertile soil. With time, nurturing, and faith, those seeds will yield a bountiful harvest. Whether you are working in your career, your family life, or your community, remember that God sees your efforts. He honors hard work and rewards those who stay committed.

Let's look at the example of Joseph. Sold into slavery by his brothers and falsely accused, he faced incredible trials. Yet, despite his circumstances, Joseph remained diligent in his work. He served faithfully in Potiphar's house, managing it with excellence. Because of his hard work and integrity, he was eventually elevated to the position of Pharaoh's right-hand man. Joseph's story teaches us that no matter how bleak our situation may seem, God can turn our labor into triumph if we remain steadfast.

Hard work often comes with sacrifices, and it requires perseverance. There will be times when you might feel like giving up, but that's when you must dig deep and remember the promises of God. Colossians 3:23-24 says, *"Whatever you do, work heartily, as for the Lord and not for men, knowing that from the Lord you will receive the inheritance as your reward."* This verse is a reminder that our efforts are not just for earthly rewards but for heavenly treasures. When we labor as if we are working for God, we align ourselves with His purpose and receive His blessings.

Moreover, the impact of our diligence extends beyond our personal gain. As we work hard and achieve success, we become a blessing to others. Our diligence can inspire those around us. Our family, friends, and coworkers take notice of our work ethic and are motivated to elevate their own standards.

This ripple effect of hard work can transform entire communities. Just as a candle can light up a dark room, your diligent efforts can shine brightly, guiding others toward their potential.

So let's not shy away from hard work. Let's accept it! Let's remember that our labor is meaningful, that we are part of a greater story, and that our diligence today is paving the way for a brighter tomorrow.

## PERSEVERING THROUGH CHALLENGES

In our walk through hard work and diligence, we will inevitably face challenges. Life is full of obstacles that can discourage us and make us want to throw in the towel. Yet, it is during these challenging moments that our true character is forged, and our commitment to hard work is tested.

Winston Churchill once said, "*Success is not final, failure is not fatal: It is the courage to continue that counts.*" These words resonate deeply, reminding us that the road to success is rarely a straight path. Instead, it is a winding journey filled with ups and downs.

In Proverbs 24:16, we read, "*For though the righteous fall seven times, they rise again, but the wicked stumble when calamity strikes.*" This scripture reveals a profound truth: resilience is an essential part of diligence. Falling down is part of the journey; getting back up is where the magic happens.

When we encounter setbacks, we must view them as opportunities for growth. Consider the story of Thomas Edison, the inventor who famously stated, "*I have not failed. I've just found 10,000 ways that won't work.*" Each failure brought him closer to success. He didn't allow setbacks to define him; instead, he used them as stepping stones toward his ultimate goal.

In your life, there will be moments that test your resolve. You may pour your heart into a project only to see it fall short of your expectations. You may work tirelessly toward a promotion, only to watch someone else take the lead. But remember, those moments are not the end of your journey—they are simply part of the process.

It's crucial to maintain your focus on the goal. As Colossians 3:23-24 encourages us, *"Whatever you do, work heartily, as for the Lord and not for men."* Keep your eyes fixed on the purpose behind your efforts. You are not just working for a paycheck or recognition; you are building a legacy, shaping your character, and fulfilling the calling God has placed on your life.

Surround yourself with inspiration. Seek out stories of those who have triumphed over adversity, who have faced challenges but pressed on with unwavering faith. As Harriet Beecher Stowe beautifully put it, *"Never give up, for that is just the place and time that the tide will turn."*

When you encounter difficulties, remember that you have the strength to persevere. Each day you show up and give your best, you are not only honoring God but also laying the groundwork for your future success. You are building a fortress of faith and resilience that will serve you well in the times to come.

So when the storms of life rage, stand firm. Hold onto your vision and continue to work diligently. Let every challenge deepen your resolve and strengthen your determination.

Your hard work is not in vain. God is watching, and He is faithful to reward those who diligently seek Him. You are planting seeds of greatness, and in due time, those seeds will blossom into a harvest beyond your wildest dreams.

## THE REWARDS OF HARD WORK

As we continue to go on about the principles of hard work and diligence, it's important to recognize that these efforts do not go unnoticed. The Bible is full of promises regarding the rewards that come from laboring with integrity and purpose. In Proverbs 14:23, we read, *"All hard work brings a profit, but mere talk leads only to poverty."* This powerful verse reminds us that the fruits of our labor are tangible and real.

When we commit ourselves to hard work, we are not only sowing seeds for our future but also cultivating a spirit of diligence that reflects God's character. As we engage in our tasks—whether at home, in the workplace, or in our communities—let us remember that we are doing more than just checking off boxes; we are building a foundation for our success.

The Parable of the Talents in Matthew 25:14-30 beautifully illustrates this principle. In the parable, a master entrusts his servants with talents—representing money or resources—before going on a journey. When he returns, he rewards those who worked diligently and multiplied what he had given them, while the servant who buried his talent out of fear is cast away. This story teaches us that God expects us to use our gifts and resources wisely and that there are consequences for our diligence or lack thereof.

The rewards of hard work extend beyond financial gain. They encompass personal growth, fulfillment, and the joy of contributing positively to the world around us. When we put in the effort, we develop skills, resilience, and character. We gain respect and build trust with those around us. As we pour our hearts into our work, we often find our passions ignited, leading us to discover new opportunities we never imagined.

Hard work is also a testament to our faith. When we labor diligently, we are expressing our belief that God honors our efforts. We show the world that we are committed to excellence in all we do. As Colossians 3:24 reminds us, *"It is the Lord Christ you are serving."*

Our work is an act of worship, a way of glorifying God and reflecting His goodness in our lives.

Let us also remember that success is not always immediate. Sometimes the rewards of our labor are delayed, requiring patience and perseverance. This is where faith truly comes into play. Hebrews 11:6 assures us that *"He rewards those who earnestly seek Him."* God sees our hard work, even when it feels like no one else does. He is faithful to bring about the increase in His perfect timing.

Consider the story of Oprah Winfrey, who overcame tremendous obstacles through hard work and resilience. From her humble beginnings, she dedicated herself to her craft, worked diligently, and never gave up on her dreams. Today, she is a media mogul and an inspiration to millions. Her story is an example to the rewards that come from hard work and unwavering commitment.

In your own life, embrace the journey, celebrating the small victories along the way, for each step is a show of your dedication and diligence. When you feel weary, remember that your hard work is a seed planted in the fertile soil of God's promise. And as you continue to cultivate that seed with faith and perseverance, it will bloom into something beautiful.

**So stand firm in your labor!** Keep your eyes on the rewards that God has promised you. He is a faithful God who honors diligence and hard work. The blessings that flow from your efforts will touch not only your life but also the lives of those around you.

## EMBRACING A DILIGENT SPIRIT

In our journey of hard work and diligence, we must cultivate a spirit that embraces every task with enthusiasm and purpose. This means approaching our responsibilities with a mindset that says, "I am not just working for myself; I am serving a higher purpose." When we see our work as an opportunity to reflect God's glory, we find fulfillment even in the most mundane tasks.

Proverbs 12:24 tells us, *"The hand of the diligent will rule, while the slothful will be put to forced labor."* This verse speaks to the power of a diligent spirit—a spirit that is proactive, eager to take on challenges, and ready to rise above the ordinary. When we embody diligence, we position ourselves as leaders in our fields, our families, and our communities.

Think about the great leaders of history, those who have made lasting impacts on our world. They did not rise to prominence by chance; they worked diligently, often sacrificing their time, comfort, and desires for a greater cause. Nelson Mandela is a powerful example of this. His unwavering commitment to justice and equality took decades of hard work and perseverance. He faced countless obstacles, yet he never wavered. His diligence and steadfast spirit ultimately changed the course of a nation.

As you pursue your dreams, remind yourself that hard work is not just a means to an end; it is part of the journey that shapes your character. Galatians 6:9 encourages us, *"Let us not become weary in doing good, for at the proper time we will reap a harvest if we do not give up."* Your consistent efforts, your dedication to doing what is right, will bear fruit. Trust in the timing of God's plan. He is the master gardener, tending to the seeds you are planting through your hard work.

In our fast-paced world, it can be easy to seek quick fixes and immediate gratification. However, the principles of diligence teach us that true success often requires time and sustained effort. Cherish the process! Each step forward, no matter how small, is a step toward your destiny. Every late night, every early morning, every moment spent honing your craft is building a foundation for your future.

To cultivate a diligent spirit, we must also guard against distractions and complacency. It's easy to get sidetracked by the noise around us or to settle for mediocrity. But when we remember that we are called to excellence, we can push through the temptation to give less than our best. Colossians 3:23-24 reminds us that whatever we do, we should work at it with all our heart, as working for the Lord.

When we embrace a diligent spirit, we create a ripple effect that can inspire those around us. Our commitment to hard work can motivate others to pursue their own dreams with vigor. You may be a beacon of light in your family, workplace, or community, encouraging others to rise up and strive for greatness.

Remember, **the race is not always to the swift** but to those who endure. Your journey may have its share of challenges, but it is in those challenges that your true character is forged. Keep your eyes on the prize, remain steadfast in your work, and trust that God will honor your diligence.

As you go forth today, embrace the spirit of hard work! Approach your tasks with joy, knowing that you are sowing seeds of greatness. Let every effort you put forth be a reflection of your commitment to excellence and a testament to your faith in God's promises.

## THE FRUIT OF DILIGENCE

Let's reflect on the abundant harvest that comes from our labor. Proverbs 14:23 states, *"In all toil there is profit, but mere talk tends only to poverty."* This verse underscores a profound truth: diligent effort yields tangible results. When we commit ourselves wholeheartedly to our tasks, we set the stage for blessings that can overflow into every area of our lives.

**The fruit of diligence is twofold**. First, it is the tangible rewards that come from our hard work. This might manifest as promotions at work, successful projects, or personal achievements. When we invest our time and energy, God often honors our commitment with visible blessings. Remember, every moment you pour into your work is an investment in your future. It may feel tedious at times, but trust that the seeds you are planting will sprout in due season.

Secondly, the fruit of diligence is spiritual. It shapes our character, fortifies our faith, and draws us closer to God. When we work diligently, we cultivate perseverance, resilience, and integrity. We learn that success is not just about the end result but the journey we take to get there. Each challenge faced, each obstacle overcome, deepens our relationship with the Lord.

Hard work fosters a mindset of gratitude and humility. As we see the fruits of our labor, we are reminded that our abilities and opportunities come from God. Colossians 3:24 encourages us that *"it is the Lord Christ you are serving."* Recognizing this truth keeps us grounded and focused. Our diligence is not merely for personal gain; it is a service to our Creator, our families, and our communities.

Let us also remember that diligence does not mean working ourselves to the bone. It is about working smart, finding balance, and maintaining our well-being. God desires that we thrive in our efforts, not be burdened by them. Matthew 11:28-30 invites us to come to Jesus for rest. In our diligent pursuit, let's not neglect the importance of taking breaks, recharging our spirits, and nurturing our relationships.

As we draw closer to our goals, celebrate the victories, big and small. Take time to acknowledge the progress you've made. Whether it's completing a project, receiving positive feedback, or simply sticking to your commitments, these moments deserve recognition. Gratitude fuels motivation and keeps us aligned with God's purpose.

Finally, share the fruits of your diligence. As you experience success, remember to lift others up along the way. Your story of hard work can inspire someone else to pursue their dreams with vigor. Proverbs 11:25 tells us, *"Whoever brings blessing will be enriched, and one who waters will himself be watered."* As you pour into others, you'll find that your own blessings multiply.

## EMBRACING A LIFE OF DILIGENCE

As we wrap up this chapter on hard work and diligence, let's take a moment to reflect on the incredible journey we've embarked upon. Remember, diligence is not just a task; it's a lifestyle—a choice we make daily to commit ourselves to excellence in everything we do. Colossians 3:23-24 reminds us that whatever we do, we should work heartily, as for the Lord and not for men. This is our guiding principle!

You see, diligence leads us to unlock doors that were once closed, to achieve what seemed impossible, and to create a life that reflects our highest potential. Every ounce of effort you invest today is paving the way for tomorrow's success. Each late night, every early morning, and all the moments of focus and determination are seeds planted in the garden of your future.

But remember this: The road to success is often paved with challenges. There may be days when you feel like giving up, when the obstacles seem insurmountable, and the end goal feels distant. In those moments, hold on to the promise of Philippians 4:13: *"I can do all things through Christ who strengthens me."* Your strength comes from a source greater than yourself. Lean into that strength, draw upon it, and let it propel you forward!

Let's also not forget the example set by those who have gone before us. Great figures throughout history have demonstrated the power of hard work and diligence. Take Maya Angelou, who once said, *"Nothing will work unless you do."* Her words echo the truth that success is not handed to us; it's earned through sweat, sacrifice, and unwavering dedication. Each of us has the potential to leave a mark on this world, but it starts with the willingness to put in the work.

So, let's make a decision today to approach every task with purpose and integrity. When you dedicate yourself to hard work, you not only change your circumstances but also inspire those around you to rise to new heights.

So here's your call to action: **Dream big, work hard, and trust in the process.** Embrace every opportunity that comes your way, no matter how small it may seem. Each task is a stepping stone leading you to your destiny. Celebrate your achievements, learn from your failures, and keep moving forward with faith.

Finally, let's carry the spirit of diligence into every aspect of our lives. May your work be a reflection of your faith, your dreams, and your God-given purpose. As you pursue your goals with hard work and diligence, know that God is with you every step of the way, guiding you, blessing you, and celebrating your successes.

**Remember, you were born for greatness!** Stand firm in your diligence, and watch as God opens doors you never imagined possible. Your future is bright, your potential is limitless, and your hard work will lead to a harvest beyond measure. Go forth and shine!

# CHAPTER 5

# Patience and Perseverance

## THE POWER OF PATIENCE AND PERSEVERANCE

In our pursuit of success, it's essential to recognize that patience and perseverance are not just virtues; they are the bedrock upon which our dreams are built. As we journey through life, we often find ourselves in a hurry—eager for the fruits of our labor to manifest, anxious for our prayers to be answered, and desperate for immediate results. Yet, the truth is that the most profound blessings often require us to wait and to endure.

James 1:3-4 reminds us, "*Because you know that the testing of your faith produces perseverance. Let perseverance finish its work so that you may be mature and complete, not lacking anything.*" Here, we see that patience is not a passive waiting; it's an active choice to trust God's timing, to believe in His promises, and to persist through challenges. It's the understanding that every delay has a purpose and that our character is being shaped in the process.

Consider the story of Joseph, who faced betrayal, imprisonment, and years of waiting before he saw the fulfillment of his dreams. Despite the hardships, Joseph remained faithful and patient, ultimately rising to a position of great influence in Egypt. His journey teaches us that perseverance through trials can lead us to unimaginable heights.

Similarly, Galatians 6:9 encourages us with the promise, "*Let us not become weary in doing good, for at the proper time we will reap a harvest if we do not give up.*" This scripture underscores the importance of steadfastness. It reminds us that success is not always about immediate gratification; often, it's about the long game.

As we see the themes of patience and perseverance in this chapter, let us go into how these qualities empower us to navigate life's uncertainties. We'll examine biblical examples that inspire us to remain steadfast in our faith, even when the road ahead seems long and winding.

In a world that often prioritizes quick results, we are called to embody a different mindset—one that embraces patience as a pathway to growth and perseverance as a symbol of our faith. Together, let's discover how cultivating these virtues can lead to a fruitful life filled with God's abundant blessings.

## CULTIVATING PATIENCE IN OUR LIVES

To cultivate patience, we must first understand that it is not merely the absence of frustration; rather, it is an active choice to remain hopeful and steadfast in our faith. Patience allows us to navigate the storms of life with grace, enabling us to respond to challenges rather than react to them.

As we consider the life of Job, we find a powerful example of patience in action. Job faced unimaginable loss and suffering, yet he refused to curse God or abandon his faith. Instead, he clung to the belief that his trials would lead to greater understanding and restoration. James 5:11 highlights this, stating, "*As you know, we consider blessed those who have persevered. You have heard of Job's perseverance and have seen what the Lord finally brought about.*" Job's story serves as a testament to the strength that comes from patiently enduring hardship.

But how do we cultivate this vital quality in our lives? It begins with a heart of gratitude. When we learn to appreciate what we have, even in times of waiting, we shift our focus from our circumstances to God's faithfulness. Philippians 4:6 encourages us, "*Do not be anxious about anything, but in every situation, by prayer and petition, with thanksgiving, present your requests to God.*" This shift in perspective transforms our waiting period into a time of preparation, growth, and deepening trust.

Moreover, we must embrace the notion that delays can be divine setups. God often uses our waiting periods to refine us, teaching us valuable lessons that will equip us for the next season of our lives. Trusting in God's timing can be challenging, especially when we feel like we are standing still while the world rushes ahead. Yet, we must remember that while we wait, God is working behind the scenes, orchestrating events and preparing us for the blessings that lie ahead.

As we reflect on our journeys, let's commit to cultivating patience, recognizing that it is not just a virtue to aspire to, but a necessary ingredient for our success. Each moment of waiting is an opportunity to strengthen our faith, deepen our character, and ultimately prepare us for the harvest that God has promised.

In this way, patience becomes more than just enduring a difficult season; it becomes a powerful tool that aligns us with God's purpose, reminding us that the journey is as important as the destination.

## THE POWER OF PERSEVERANCE

Perseverance is the relentless spirit that pushes us to continue moving forward, even when obstacles seem insurmountable. It is the determination to keep pressing on, knowing that every step brings us closer to our goals, and it is rooted deeply in our faith. When we pair patience with perseverance, we create a formidable force that propels us toward success.

The Apostle Paul beautifully illustrates this in Galatians 6:9: *"Let us not become weary in doing good, for at the proper time we will reap a harvest if we do not give up."* This scripture reminds us that our efforts are not in vain. Every act of diligence, every moment spent in prayer, and every trial we face is part of a divine plan that leads to a bountiful harvest.

Consider the story of Thomas Edison again, a man whose perseverance changed the world. He famously stated, *"I have not failed. I've just found 10,000 ways that won't work."* His unwavering commitment to his vision, despite countless setbacks, is a testament to the power of perseverance. Edison's journey teaches us that the path to success is often fraught with challenges, but it is through these challenges that we develop the strength and resilience needed to achieve our dreams.

Moreover, it's essential to remember that perseverance is not a solo journey. Surrounding ourselves with a supportive community can make all the difference. Proverbs 27:17 states, *"As iron sharpens iron, so one person sharpens another."* We are designed to uplift and encourage one another. In times of difficulty, lean on your friends, family, or mentors. Share your struggles and allow them to remind you of your strength and potential. Together, you can inspire each other to keep pushing forward.

Furthermore, our perseverance has a ripple effect on those around us. When we stand firm in our faith and continue to strive for our goals, we become beacons of hope for others. They witness our determination and are inspired to cultivate that same spirit in their own lives. Remember, your journey is not just about you; it's about the impact you make on others.

As we forge ahead, let's embrace the challenges we face as opportunities for growth. With every setback, there is a lesson to be learned. With every disappointment, there is a chance to strengthen our resolve. We must remind ourselves that true success is often birthed from perseverance and patience, and through these qualities, we align ourselves with God's perfect timing and plan.

In the words of Helen Keller, "*Alone we can do so little; together we can do so much.*" Let us commit to persevering through our trials and supporting one another on this incredible journey of faith. As we cultivate both patience and perseverance, we will not only reach our destination but do so with a spirit of gratitude and a heart full of joy.

## EMBRACING THE JOURNEY

Patience and perseverance are not just traits to be admired; they are essential qualities that help us navigate life's challenges and celebrate our victories. They teach us that success is not merely a destination but a journey filled with experiences that shape who we are. Each step we take, whether forward or backward, is a part of our story, leading us toward the fulfillment of our purpose.

James 1:3-4 reminds us of the value of this journey: *"Because you know that the testing of your faith produces perseverance. Let perseverance finish its work so that you may be mature and complete, not lacking anything."* Here, we see that patience and perseverance have a divine purpose—they refine us. Each challenge we encounter helps us grow stronger and more resilient. In this way, our trials become a classroom, teaching us lessons we would not learn in times of ease.

It's crucial to embrace the journey, no matter how difficult it may seem. Think of a caterpillar that must endure a period of struggle within its cocoon. If it were to be helped out prematurely, it would never develop the strength needed to become a butterfly. In the same way, our struggles often serve as the very catalyst for our transformation. God is working in the background, preparing us for a breakthrough that is beyond what we can imagine.

In times of doubt or frustration, remember that patience is a form of faith in action. It's about trusting that God is at work even when we cannot see the results. As we persevere, we often find that the answers we seek come in ways we did not expect. It might be a new opportunity, a shift in perspective, or a connection with someone who can help us along the way.

Let's take a moment to reflect on the words of Ralph Waldo Emerson: *"The only person you are destined to become is the person you decide to be."* Each decision we make, rooted in patience and perseverance, shapes our destiny. When we choose to persist in the face of adversity, we are actively participating in the creation of our future.

Moreover, it's essential to cultivate a mindset that celebrates small victories. Each step forward, no matter how minor it may seem, is a testament to our commitment to persevere. Celebrate these moments! They serve as reminders that progress is being made, even if it feels slow at times.

As we accept our journeys with patience and perseverance, let us also cultivate an attitude of gratitude. Gratitude allows us to focus on the positive aspects of our situations, helping us maintain perspective even in tough times. By acknowledging what we are thankful for, we create space for joy and hope, empowering us to keep moving forward.

In the end, remember that every trial you face is an opportunity for growth. Patience and perseverance are not just skills to develop; they are spiritual principles that align us with God's purpose. As you continue your journey, lean into these qualities. Let them guide you, uplift you, and remind you that your story is far from over. Your greatest triumphs are often born from the toughest battles, so keep the faith and persevere—your breakthrough is on the horizon!

## THE FRUIT OF PATIENCE AND PERSEVERANCE

As we explore the profound impact of patience and perseverance, it's important to recognize that these qualities bear fruit in our lives. The trials we endure and the steadfastness we exhibit are not in vain; they cultivate character, strengthen our resolve, and prepare us for the abundant life God has promised us.

James 1:4 declares, *"Let perseverance finish its work so that you may be mature and complete, not lacking anything."* This scripture highlights a powerful truth: patience and perseverance are integral to our spiritual and personal development. They shape our character and equip us with the tools needed to face future challenges. As we learn to wait on God and remain steadfast in our pursuits, we are not merely enduring; we are growing.

Consider the example of a farmer who plants seeds. The seeds do not sprout overnight. The farmer must water, nurture, and protect them through the changing seasons, often waiting patiently for the harvest. Galatians 6:9 encourages us with the reminder that *"in due season we will reap if we do not give up."* The harvest is the reward for diligence, hard work, and unwavering faith. Just like the farmer, we too must remain committed to our goals, knowing that our efforts will yield results in God's perfect timing.

This principle of sowing and reaping transcends physical labor and applies to every area of our lives, including relationships, career aspirations, and personal growth. When we invest time and energy into our dreams and aspirations, we are planting seeds of success. However, this process often requires us to endure setbacks, disappointments, and moments of uncertainty.

Patience teaches us to trust in the timing of God. It reminds us that while we may have our plans, His plans are always better. Isaiah 55:8-9 tells us, *"For my thoughts are not your thoughts, neither are your ways my ways... As the heavens are higher than the earth, so are my ways higher than your ways and my thoughts than your thoughts."* When we find ourselves frustrated by delays, let us remember that God sees the bigger picture. He knows the perfect time for our breakthroughs and blessings.

Perseverance, on the other hand, instills resilience in our spirits. It empowers us to rise each time we fall and encourages us to keep pushing forward, even when the odds seem stacked against us. The apostle Paul exemplified this perseverance as he faced numerous trials, shipwrecks, and imprisonments. Yet, he declared in Philippians 4:13, *"I can do all things through Christ who strengthens me."* His unwavering determination to fulfill his calling serves as a powerful reminder that we are not alone in our struggles.

As we cultivate patience and perseverance, we also learn to inspire others. Our journeys become testimonies of hope and encouragement for those around us. When others see our commitment to stay the course, even in adversity, it ignites a spark of faith within them. They begin to believe that if we can overcome challenges, so can they.

Let us take heart in knowing that our perseverance is not only for ourselves but also for those who look to us for inspiration. As we walk this path, let us be mindful of how our actions and attitudes impact others. By living out our faith with patience and perseverance, we embody the essence of Christ's love and grace, shining as lights in a world that often feels dark and discouraging.

In summary, the fruit of patience and perseverance is profound and multifaceted. It enriches our character, deepens our faith, and prepares us for the blessings ahead. Embrace the process, celebrate the growth, and trust that every step you take brings you closer to the fulfillment of God's promises. Your journey is uniquely yours, filled with lessons, victories, and divine purpose. Keep persevering, for your harvest is on its way!

## EMBRACING THE JOURNEY OF PATIENCE AND PERSEVERANCE

Patience isn't a passive state; it's an active choice. It requires us to engage with our circumstances and confront our desires with faith and hope. The journey often involves waiting—not just waiting in silence, but waiting with expectation. Psalm 27:14 reminds us, *"Wait for the Lord; be strong, and let your heart take courage; wait for the Lord!"* This verse encourages us to approach our waiting periods with strength and courage, trusting that God is working behind the scenes, orchestrating our lives according to His divine plan.

In our culture, where instant gratification is the norm, it can be easy to overlook the beauty of waiting. But think of the greatest things in life: love, success, fulfillment—these are rarely achieved overnight. They require time, effort, and a commitment to the process. Consider how diamonds are formed; they are the result of intense pressure and heat over time. In the same way, our patience under pressure leads to the development of our character, producing something precious and valuable.

Perseverance, too, is not simply about stubbornly pushing through difficulties. It's about resilience—a refusal to be defined by setbacks. When we encounter challenges, we must remember that they are not roadblocks but stepping stones on our journey to greatness. Romans 5:3-4 reminds us, *"Not only that, but we rejoice in our sufferings, knowing that suffering produces endurance, and endurance produces character, and character produces hope."* Every struggle contributes to our story, adding depth and richness to our lives.

Embracing this journey means recognizing that each moment of patience and every act of perseverance are opportunities for growth. They challenge us to rise above our circumstances and to lean into our faith. When we commit to this journey, we learn to celebrate small victories and find joy in the process. We learn that every time we choose to remain steadfast, we are building a foundation for our future.

Moreover, patience and perseverance help us cultivate gratitude. In moments of waiting, we can reflect on what we have rather than what we lack. A heart of gratitude shifts our focus from our trials to the blessings that surround us. 1 Thessalonians 5:18 encourages us, *"Give thanks in all circumstances; for this is the will of God in Christ Jesus for you."* Gratitude nurtures our spirit, allowing us to see the hand of God in every situation, big or small.

As we go through life's challenges, let us remember that we are not alone in our struggles. The great cloud of witnesses, as described in Hebrews 12:1, surrounds us, cheering us on as we run our race. They remind us that patience and perseverance are integral parts of the human experience, shared by all who have come before us.

Take heart! As you face your own mountains of challenges, remember that you have the strength to climb them. God is with you every step of the way, ready to provide the strength you need to endure. Every moment of waiting, every ounce of perseverance is a testament to your faith and commitment to the journey.

So, you see, embracing patience and perseverance is a powerful choice that leads to growth, character development, and a deeper connection with God. Each moment spent waiting is not wasted; it is a sacred opportunity to trust, to learn, and to prepare for the blessings ahead. Keep your eyes fixed on the prize, knowing that every effort you make today will pave the way for tomorrow's success. Remember, your journey is uniquely designed for you, and your breakthrough is just around the corner!

As we wrap up our exploration of patience and perseverance, let's take a moment to reflect on the profound truths we've uncovered. Life, with its twists and turns, challenges and triumphs, is a journey crafted by a loving God who desires nothing but the best for us. In every moment of waiting, in every struggle, there is a lesson, a purpose, and a chance for growth.

God's timing is perfect. Often, we find ourselves in seasons of waiting, feeling as though our dreams are just out of reach. Yet, in those moments, God is preparing us. He's refining our character, strengthening us, and deepening our faith. Isaiah 40:31 assures us, *"But those who hope in the Lord will renew their strength. They will soar on wings like eagles; they will run and not grow weary, they will walk and not be faint."* This scripture is a beautiful reminder that waiting on God is not wasted time; it's an opportunity for renewal and growth.

So, dear friend, take heart! Embrace the journey with faith, knowing that patience and perseverance are the keys to unlocking the doors of your future. Allow the seeds of hope to take root in your heart and watch as they grow into a flourishing harvest of blessings. With God by your side, there's nothing you cannot achieve. You are destined for greatness—now go and claim it!

## CHAPTER 6

# Wisdom and Discernment

### THE FOUNDATION OF WISDOM

One of the most invaluable treasures we can seek is wisdom. Proverbs 2:6 tells us, *"For the Lord gives wisdom; from His mouth comes knowledge and understanding."* This verse reminds us that wisdom is not merely a product of our experiences or education but a divine gift that comes from God Himself. It's the kind of wisdom that empowers us to navigate life's complexities with grace and clarity.

Wisdom is the ability to see the big picture, to understand the right course of action, and to make decisions that align with God's will. It is a guiding light that illuminates our path, allowing us to discern what is true, right, and beneficial. This is not just a matter of being smart or knowledgeable; it's about possessing a heart that seeks after God and His purposes.

In our fast-paced world, filled with information and distractions, it's easy to lose sight of what truly matters. However, when we prioritize seeking wisdom, we align ourselves with God's design for our lives. This pursuit begins with humility. Proverbs 11:2 states, *"When pride comes, then comes disgrace, but with humility comes wisdom."* Recognizing that we don't have all the answers is the first step toward gaining insight that transcends our understanding.

So, how do we cultivate this foundation of wisdom? It starts with a willingness to learn and grow. We must approach life with a teachable spirit, ready to absorb the lessons that God presents to us through His Word, our experiences, and the people He places in our lives. By embracing a mindset of curiosity and openness, we can invite wisdom into our hearts and minds.

Let us remember that God's desire is for us to live fully and abundantly. He longs to provide us with the insight we need to make decisions that honor Him and lead us to success. With each step we take in this journey, we can trust that God is eager to share His wisdom with those who earnestly seek it.

In the following sections, we will discover the critical role of discernment, the importance of seeking wisdom through prayer, and how the Holy Spirit can guide us in our decision-making. Together, let's unlock the treasure trove of wisdom that God has in store for us, knowing that it will lead us to a fulfilling and purposeful life.

## THE JOURNEY OF WISDOM

Let us see the story of a young man named Michael. Michael was ambitious and driven, eager to make his mark on the world. Fresh out of college, he landed a promising job at a prestigious firm. He was excited but soon found himself overwhelmed by the fast-paced environment and the expectations placed upon him.

One day, his manager presented him with a significant project that could lead to a major promotion. Michael felt the pressure mounting, and while he was tempted to jump in with both feet, he paused to consider his options. Realizing he had never faced a challenge of this magnitude before, he decided to seek wisdom before diving in headfirst.

He remembered his grandmother's advice, which echoed in his mind: "When in doubt, pray." Michael had grown up in a family that valued faith, but in his pursuit of success, he had neglected to stay connected with God. So, he took a moment in the quiet of his office, closed his eyes, and prayed for guidance. He asked for wisdom to handle the project effectively and discernment to make the right decisions.

The next morning, he opened his Bible and came across James 1:5, which states, *"If any of you lacks wisdom, let him ask of God, who gives to all liberally and without reproach, and it will be given to him."* That verse sparked something within him. He felt encouraged and understood that wisdom was available to him, not just for the project but for every aspect of his life.

As Michael began to work on the project, he approached each decision with a new perspective. He sought input from his colleagues, listened carefully to their insights, and weighed the pros and cons thoughtfully. Instead of rushing through the tasks, he took the time to research and gather information, allowing wisdom to guide his choices.

During this process, he faced a critical decision: a key aspect of the project required him to choose between cutting corners to meet the deadline or doing the job right, which would take more time and effort. The pressure was intense, and he could feel the weight of his ambition pushing him toward the shortcut. However, he paused again, remembering the importance of integrity and honesty, which he had learned in previous chapters. He knew that choosing the right path was more important than immediate success.

Michael decided to take the longer route, putting in the extra work and ensuring the project was done correctly. In the end, his decision to prioritize quality over speed earned him the respect of his team and the admiration of his superiors. His project not only met the deadline but also exceeded expectations, showcasing his commitment to excellence.

Through this experience, Michael learned that wisdom isn't just about knowledge or quick decision-making;

it's about aligning our choices with our values and God's purpose for our lives. By seeking God's guidance, he discovered the profound truth of Proverbs 2:6, that the Lord indeed gives wisdom, and from His mouth comes knowledge and understanding.

As we navigate our own paths, let Michael's story remind us that seeking wisdom and discernment leads to a fulfilling and purposeful life. With each decision we face, let's pause, pray, and invite God into the process. By doing so, we will unlock the wisdom that helps us rise above challenges and align our lives with His divine plan.

## THE PURSUIT OF WISDOM

The journey of life is filled with decisions that shape our future. As we strive to embrace wisdom and discernment in our daily lives, it's essential to recognize the profound impact they have on our decisions. Wisdom is not merely about accumulating knowledge; it's about applying that knowledge in a way that reflects our values and aligns with God's will.

Let's take a moment to reflect on a biblical figure known for his extraordinary wisdom: King Solomon.

When Solomon became king, he was faced with the monumental task of leading a nation. Overwhelmed by the responsibility, he sought God's guidance and asked for wisdom to govern His people. In response, God granted him unparalleled wisdom, making him one of the wisest leaders in history.

One of the most famous stories illustrating Solomon's wisdom is the case of two women who came to him, each claiming to be the mother of a baby. The situation was dire, and emotions ran high as they argued over the child. Solomon, known for his discerning spirit, proposed a solution: he suggested dividing the baby in two, giving half to each woman. While this seemed cruel, it revealed the truth. The real mother immediately offered to give up her claim to save her child, demonstrating her genuine love and selflessness.

Solomon's ability to discern the truth amidst a complex situation not only saved the child's life but also established his reputation as a wise and just king. This story reminds us that true wisdom often involves difficult decisions and the courage to choose what is right over what is easy. Solomon's example encourages us to seek discernment in our own lives, especially in challenging situations.

So, how can we cultivate this spirit of wisdom and discernment? The answer lies in a few key practices:

1. **Seek God First:** In all our endeavors, we should prioritize seeking God's will. Before making significant decisions, pray and ask for guidance. James 1:5 reassures us that when we seek wisdom, God will generously provide it. Create a habit of starting your day with prayer, inviting God into your plans.
2. **Study the Word:** The Bible is a treasure trove of wisdom. Regularly reading and meditating on scripture equips us with the knowledge needed to navigate life's complexities. Proverbs 2:6 reminds us that the Lord gives wisdom, and His words are our guide. By immersing ourselves in God's Word, we sharpen our discernment and enhance our ability to make sound decisions.
3. **Surround Yourself with Wise Counsel:** As Michael did in the earlier story, surround yourself with individuals who possess wisdom and discernment. Seek mentors, friends, or spiritual leaders who can offer valuable insights. Proverbs 15:22 tells us that *"plans fail for lack of counsel, but with many*

*advisers, they succeed."* Engaging with wise counsel can provide clarity and perspective when we face tough choices.

4. **Practice Patience:** In our fast-paced world, it's easy to rush into decisions without fully considering the consequences. However, wisdom often requires us to pause and reflect. In moments of uncertainty, remind yourself of James 1:3-4, which teaches us that the testing of our faith produces perseverance. Embrace the process and allow patience to cultivate wisdom within you.

5. **Learn from Experience:** Every decision we make is an opportunity for growth. Reflect on past choices—both successful and unsuccessful. Ask yourself what you learned from each experience. This reflection not only deepens our understanding but also prepares us for future challenges. Remember, wisdom is often born from our trials and errors.

In our pursuit of wisdom, we must recognize that it is a journey rather than a destination. Each day presents new opportunities to seek, learn, and apply wisdom in our lives. As we navigate through life's decisions, let us strive to be like Solomon, drawing on God's guidance to illuminate our path and empower us to make choices that honor Him.

In the next part, we will explore the transformative power of discernment and how it can help us navigate the complexities of our relationships, careers, and personal lives. So let's keep our hearts open and our spirits attuned to the wisdom that God offers us every day.

## THE TRANSFORMATIVE POWER OF DISCERNMENT

As we continue our exploration of wisdom and discernment, it's crucial to recognize the transformative power of discernment in our lives. Discernment is the ability to perceive and understand things clearly; it's about seeing beyond the surface and grasping the deeper truths. In a world filled with noise and confusion, discernment becomes our spiritual compass, guiding us toward the right path and helping us make decisions that align with God's purpose for our lives.

Imagine a young woman named Sarah, who faced a significant career decision. She had two job offers: one at a prestigious company with a high salary and another at a non-profit organization that aligned with her passion for helping others. On the surface, the high-paying job seemed like the better choice, offering financial stability and security. However, Sarah felt a tug in her heart toward the non-profit role. It was a place where she could make a genuine impact and fulfill her calling.

In moments of uncertainty, Sarah turned to prayer and sought God's guidance. She remembered James 1:5, which promises that if we ask for wisdom, God will give it generously. After praying and reflecting on her values, she realized that her true desire was to serve and uplift those in need. With this newfound clarity, Sarah made the decision to accept the non-profit position. Although it meant sacrificing a higher salary, she found joy and fulfillment in her work, knowing she was contributing to a cause she deeply believed in.

Sarah's story highlights the significance of discernment in making decisions that resonate with our values and calling. It's easy to be swayed by societal expectations or the allure of worldly success, but true discernment helps us stay aligned with our purpose. When we cultivate discernment, we develop the ability to assess situations, weigh our options, and choose the path that best reflects God's will for our lives.

## THE ROLE OF DISCERNMENT IN RELATIONSHIPS

Discernment is not limited to career choices; it also plays a vital role in our relationships. The people we surround ourselves with can significantly influence our spiritual journey and overall well-being. Proverbs 13:20 reminds us that *"walk with the wise and become wise, for a companion of fools suffers harm."* By exercising discernment in our relationships, we can foster connections that uplift us and steer clear of those that may lead us astray.

Consider the story of Michael again. After gaining wisdom from his earlier experiences, he realized the importance of surrounding himself with people who shared his values and aspirations. He began to intentionally invest in friendships with individuals who encouraged him in his faith and motivated him to grow. These relationships not only strengthened his resolve but also provided him with a support system during challenging times.

In contrast, Michael also recognized the need to distance himself from toxic relationships that drained his energy and discouraged his progress. This wasn't an easy choice, but he understood that discernment meant making tough decisions for his well-being. By prioritizing relationships that aligned with his values, he was able to cultivate a circle of support that encouraged his spiritual growth and fueled his passion for serving others.

## DISCERNMENT IN DAILY LIFE

Discernment extends to our daily choices as well. From how we spend our time to the media we consume, every decision we make has the potential to shape our character and spiritual journey. By practicing discernment in our everyday lives, we can align our actions with God's will.

**Here are a few practical steps to develop discernment in your daily choices:**

1. **Evaluate Your Priorities**: Take time to assess what truly matters in your life. Are your daily activities aligning with your core values and goals? Reflecting on your priorities can help you make intentional choices that reflect your commitment to God's purpose.
2. **Limit Distractions**: In our fast-paced world, it's easy to become overwhelmed by distractions. Set boundaries around technology and social media to create space for prayer, reflection, and connecting with God. This intentional focus will enhance your ability to discern what truly matters.
3. **Practice Gratitude**: Cultivating a spirit of gratitude can shift your perspective and enhance your discernment. When you focus on the blessings in your life, you develop a deeper appreciation for God's guidance and provision. This mindset can empower you to make choices rooted in thankfulness and trust.
4. **Seek Confirmation:** When faced with significant decisions, don't hesitate to seek

confirmation from trusted mentors or spiritual leaders. Their insights can provide clarity and reassurance as you navigate complex choices.

5. **Trust Your Instincts**: Often, God speaks to us through our instincts and inner promptings. Pay attention to those nudges that guide you toward certain decisions. Trust that God is leading you, and embrace the discernment He provides.

As we embrace the power of discernment, we gain the ability to navigate life's complexities with confidence. Like Sarah and Michael, we can make choices that align with our values, deepen our relationships, and fulfill our divine purpose. In the next section, we'll explore how wisdom and discernment work together, equipping us to face challenges and pursue our God-given dreams. Let's open our hearts to the transformative journey that lies ahead!

## THE SYNERGY OF WISDOM AND DISCERNMENT

As we conclude our exploration of wisdom and discernment, it's essential to recognize how these two principles work hand in hand. Wisdom is the foundation, while discernment is the lens through which we see our circumstances. Together, they empower us to make choices that not only reflect our values but also align with God's divine plan for our lives.

When we seek wisdom, we are asking for a deeper understanding of God's will and the ability to navigate the complexities of life with grace. It allows us to see the bigger picture and recognize the potential consequences of our actions. Discernment, on the other hand, sharpens our ability to evaluate specific situations, helping us to sift through options and make choices that lead us closer to our goals.

When we look at the story of Daniel in the Bible, as a young man, Daniel was taken captive in Babylon and faced numerous challenges that tested his faith and integrity. Yet, he consistently sought God's wisdom through prayer and remained discerning in his interactions with the king and his court. His commitment to God allowed him to excel in his position, and his discernment led to opportunities that ultimately changed the course of nations. Daniel's life illustrates the profound impact of combining wisdom with discernment, showcasing how one can thrive even in the most challenging circumstances.

In our lives, we may encounter times of uncertainty or decision-making that feel overwhelming. However, when we anchor ourselves in God's wisdom and cultivate our discernment, we can face these moments with confidence. By leaning on scripture and seeking guidance through prayer, we equip ourselves to make decisions that honor God and further our purpose.

Today, I invite you to embrace wisdom and discernment as essential tools in your spiritual toolkit. Remember, seeking wisdom is not a one-time event but a lifelong pursuit. Make it a habit to turn to scripture, to seek wise counsel, and to engage in prayerful reflection. In doing so, you will cultivate a heart that is open to God's guidance and responsive to the whispers of the Holy Spirit.

In moments when you feel uncertain, remind yourself of the promise found in James 1:5: *"If any of you lacks wisdom, let him ask of God, who gives to all liberally and without reproach, and it will be given to him."* God is eager to provide the wisdom you seek; all you need to do is ask.

As you step on, keep this quote close to your heart: *"Wisdom is not the product of schooling but of the lifelong attempt to acquire it."* — Albert Einstein.

Let this serve as a reminder that the pursuit of wisdom and discernment is a journey, not a destination. Embrace the process, and you will find that every step taken in faith brings you closer to the abundant life God has promised you. Trust in His guidance, and may your life be a show of the power of living with wisdom and discernment. Amen!

# CHAPTER 7

# Gratitude and Contentment

## THE POWER OF GRATITUDE

Gratitude is a game-changer. It's more than just saying "thank you" when things go our way. It's about maintaining a heart of thankfulness in every season—when the sun is shining, but also when the clouds roll in. Gratitude has a way of shifting our perspective and helping us to see God's hand at work, even when life seems tough.

Many people struggle with staying positive because they focus too much on what they don't have. They see the obstacles, the lack, the delay in answered prayers. But the truth is, God has already given us so much to be thankful for. The very breath in our lungs, the ability to wake up each day, our family, our friends—these are all blessings that we sometimes overlook. Gratitude is about shifting our focus from what's missing to what's present, from what we lack to what we already have.

Paul tells us in 1 Thessalonians 5:18 to *"give thanks in all circumstances; for this is God's will for you in Christ Jesus."* He didn't say give thanks only when everything is going great. He said in all circumstances. That means in the highs and the lows, the victories and the challenges, we are called to be grateful. When we start seeing life through a lens of gratitude, it's amazing how things begin to change. What once felt like a burden starts to feel like a blessing.

Think about it. When you focus on gratitude, you activate a new level of faith. You remind yourself that God is still in control, that He's still working things out for your good. You may not have everything you want right now, but you can thank God that He's preparing something even greater in the future. Gratitude helps us to recognize that God's plans are always bigger than our own.

I once heard a story about a man who lost his job unexpectedly. He had a choice—he could either focus on his loss and spiral into despair, or he could turn to God with a heart full of gratitude. Despite his disappointment, he chose to thank God for all the years of employment he had enjoyed, for his family's health, and for the new opportunities that he trusted were on the horizon. In the end, not only did God bless him with a new job, but one that was far better than the one he had lost. That's the power of gratitude—it positions us to receive even more of God's blessings.

So today, start practicing gratitude. Take time to thank God for the blessings in your life, both big and small. Let go of what you think is missing and trust that God is working all things together for your good. You'll find that when your heart is full of thankfulness, your spirit is lifted, your faith grows stronger, and you begin to live with a deep sense of contentment in every area of your life.

## CONTENTMENT IN ALL CIRCUMSTANCES

Contentment is not about having everything you want, but about recognizing the blessing in what you have.

In a world that constantly tells us to reach for more, to climb higher, and to never be satisfied, contentment is a powerful spiritual discipline. It's the ability to say, *"I have enough, because God has already given me more than I deserve."*

Now, don't misunderstand—there's nothing wrong with having ambition, with setting goals, and pursuing dreams. God desires that we live abundant, fulfilling lives. But here's the key: while you're reaching for your goals, don't let discontentment rob you of the joy of the present moment. God wants us to live with a balance—striving for better while being at peace with where we are right now.

Hebrews 13:5 tells us, *"Keep your lives free from the love of money and be content with what you have, because God has said, 'Never will I leave you; never will I forsake you.'"* This verse highlights a truth that we can sometimes overlook: contentment is rooted in trust. It's trusting that God is with us, providing for us, and guiding us. If we're constantly yearning for more, we're essentially saying that what God has given us isn't enough. But when we practice contentment, we're saying, *"Lord, I trust You. I trust that You've given* me what I need in this season, and I trust that You will provide more when the time is right."

One of the greatest examples of contentment comes from the Apostle Paul. In Philippians 4:11-12, he says, *"I have learned to be content whatever the circumstances. I know what it is to be in need, and I know what it is to have plenty. I have learned the secret of being content in any and every situation, whether well fed or hungry, whether living in plenty or in want."* Paul's contentment wasn't tied to his circumstances. Whether he was in a season of abundance or in a time of lack, his joy and peace remained intact because his contentment was anchored in God, not in his material situation.

Here's the beautiful thing about contentment—it sets you free. When you're content, you're no longer chasing after things that don't matter. You're no longer comparing your life to someone else's. You stop measuring your worth by what you have or don't have. Instead, you find peace in knowing that God has you right where He wants you. That doesn't mean your situation won't change—it just means you won't let your situation steal your joy in the meantime.

Let me share a story with you. There was a woman who had been waiting for years to start a family. She and her husband had prayed and hoped, but month after month, there was no baby. She had a choice: she could live in frustration and disappointment, or she could choose to be content and trust that God had a plan. She decided to live in contentment, focusing on the blessings in her life, like her marriage, her friends, and her faith. One day, without warning, she found out she was pregnant. But here's the point—her joy didn't start with the pregnancy; her joy was already there, rooted in her contentment with God.

When we find contentment in God, we begin to experience true freedom. We're no longer bound by the need to accumulate more, to achieve more, or to impress others. We live in the peace of knowing that God has given us exactly what we need for today, and that tomorrow's blessings will come in His perfect timing.

## GRATITUDE IN EVERY SEASON

Gratitude is more than just saying "thank you" when something good happens—it's a way of life. It's a mindset that acknowledges God's hand in every detail, every blessing, and every trial. In 1 Thessalonians 5:18, we are instructed, *"Give thanks in all circumstances; for this is God's will for you in Christ Jesus."* Notice that it says *"in all circumstances."* It doesn't say to give thanks only when things are going well. It's a call to gratitude even in the difficult times.

Why is this so important? Because gratitude shifts your perspective. When you start looking for things to be thankful for, even in the hardest moments, you begin to see the world differently. What might have seemed like a setback now becomes an opportunity to witness God's provision. What felt like a loss can become a lesson in God's faithfulness. The more you give thanks, the more you recognize how much you truly have to be thankful for.

Think about the story of the Israelites in the wilderness. God had just freed them from slavery in Egypt, performed miracles, and promised them a land flowing with milk and honey. But instead of gratitude, many of them chose to complain. They focused on what they didn't have instead of the miraculous deliverance God had already provided. Their lack of gratitude led to wandering in the wilderness for forty years. It wasn't because God couldn't take them to the promised land sooner—it was because their hearts weren't ready to receive it.

Sometimes, we too can get stuck in our own wilderness when we focus on what's missing instead of what's been given. But when we choose gratitude, even when the situation is less than perfect, we position ourselves for God's blessing. Gratitude opens the door for God to work in our lives in ways we can't even imagine.

A pastor once told the story of a man who lost everything—his job, his home, and most of his possessions. Instead of spiraling into despair, this man made a decision: every day, he would find one thing to be grateful for. Some days, it was something as simple as the sunrise or a warm cup of coffee. Over time, his attitude shifted. Even though his circumstances were tough, his heart was full of gratitude, and that kept his spirit alive. Eventually, God restored him, giving him more than he had lost, but it was his gratitude in the storm that truly transformed him.

The key to gratitude is understanding that it's not dependent on what you have, but on who you have. When your trust is in God, you realize that He is more than enough. You begin to see that every blessing, whether big or small, is a reflection of His goodness. You stop worrying about what's next and start appreciating what's now.

Here's the truth: there's always something to be grateful for. If you have breath in your lungs, you have a reason to give thanks. If you woke up this morning, that's another reason. Gratitude is not about denying the difficulties—it's about recognizing that even in those difficulties, God is still good. It's about acknowledging that He is working all things together for your good, even when you can't see it yet.

One of the most powerful ways to practice gratitude is through prayer. When you start your prayers with thanksgiving, it changes the whole atmosphere. Instead of coming to God with a list of requests, you come with a heart full of appreciation. You begin to see that He's already working in ways you didn't notice before. That's why Paul writes in Philippians 4:6, *"Do not be anxious about anything, but in every situation, by prayer and petition, with thanksgiving, present your requests to God."* Thanksgiving is the foundation of faith-filled prayer. It's the acknowledgment that God has already been faithful and will continue to be faithful.

Living a life of gratitude doesn't mean ignoring life's challenges. It means choosing to see God's hand in the midst of those challenges. It's about trusting that He is enough, that He is working on your behalf, and that He is leading you exactly where you need to go. Gratitude keeps you grounded in that truth.

## CONTENTMENT IN GOD'S PROVISION

While gratitude is about recognizing the blessings we already have, contentment is about being at peace with where we are in life. Contentment says, *"I trust that God knows what I need, and I'm satisfied in His provision."* It's not passive acceptance, but an active choice to rest in God's timing and plan.

Hebrews 13:5 gives us a powerful reminder: *"Keep your lives free from the love of money and be content with what you have, because God has said, 'Never will I leave you; never will I forsake you.'"* Contentment is grounded in the knowledge that God is with us, that He sees our needs, and that He provides everything we need—not necessarily everything we want, but what we need to fulfill His purpose in our lives.

In today's world, contentment can feel like a foreign concept. We are constantly bombarded with messages telling us we need more: a bigger house, a better job, more status, more recognition. But God's kingdom operates on a different principle. True contentment isn't found in what we have or what we achieve—it's found in our relationship with God.

The Apostle Paul understood this better than anyone. In Philippians 4:11-12, he writes, *"I have learned to be content whatever the circumstances. I know what it is to be in need, and I know what it is to have plenty. I have learned the secret of being content in any and every situation."* Paul had been through highs and lows, but he learned that contentment wasn't about his external circumstances. It was about his internal peace, rooted in his faith in God.

Contentment doesn't mean that we stop dreaming or striving for more, but it does mean that we trust God with the process. We don't need to chase after every opportunity out of fear of missing out. We don't need to compare our lives to others or feel inadequate because we're not where we thought we'd be. Contentment says, "I trust that God has me exactly where I need to be at this moment."

Let's look at a short story that illustrates this. There was once a fisherman who lived a simple life by the sea. Every day, he would catch just enough fish to feed his family and a few neighbors. One day, a wealthy businessman approached him and said, *"Why don't you catch more fish? You could sell them and make more money."*

The fisherman asked, *"What would I do with the extra money?"*

The businessman replied, *"You could buy a bigger boat, hire some workers, and expand your business."*

*"And then what?"* asked the fisherman.

*"Well, with time, you could become the richest man in the village, maybe even in the entire region,"* the businessman said.

*"And after that?"*

*"Then, you could retire and spend your days relaxing by the sea,"* the businessman concluded.

The fisherman smiled and said, *"But I'm already doing that."*

The fisherman's contentment wasn't in the size of his business or how much wealth he could accumulate. It was in the peace and joy he found in his daily life, doing what he loved, and being with the people he cared about. He understood that more doesn't always mean better.

In the same way, we can learn to be content in whatever season we find ourselves. Maybe you're in a season of waiting, where it feels like your prayers haven't been answered yet. Contentment doesn't mean giving up on those prayers, but it does mean trusting that God's timing is perfect. It means recognizing that even in the waiting, God is working on your behalf. He's preparing you for what's ahead, and He's providing for your needs right now.

When we practice contentment, we are freed from the constant striving and stressing that so often drains our joy. We learn to enjoy the present moment, to appreciate the blessings we already have, and to trust that God's plans are good, even when we can't see the full picture.

## LIVING A LIFE OF GRATITUDE AND CONTENTMENT

As we wrap up this chapter on gratitude and contentment, it's important to understand that these principles are not just temporary feelings, but a way of life. When you commit to living with a heart full of gratitude and contentment, you shift your focus from what the world says you lack to the abundance God has already given you. You begin to walk in the peace and joy that comes from knowing you are in the center of God's plan.

Think about the story of the Israelites in the wilderness. Despite God providing for them daily—manna from heaven, water from a rock—they grumbled and complained because their eyes were set on what they didn't have. They wanted more, and in doing so, they missed out on the fullness of the blessings right in front of them.

How often do we fall into that same trap? We overlook the countless ways God is working in our lives because we're focused on what we wish we had or where we think we should be. But living in gratitude and contentment helps us to appreciate what we have, trusting that God is faithful to bring us what we need, when we need it.

1 Thessalonians 5:18 commands us, *"Give thanks in all circumstances; for this is God's will for you in Christ Jesus."* This verse doesn't say to give thanks for all circumstances, but in all circumstances. Whether you're on the mountaintop or walking through the valley, God is with you, and His goodness never changes. When we embrace this truth, we can truly say, *"It is well with my soul."*

Remember, contentment isn't settling for less—it's trusting that God's provision is enough. It's about being satisfied in Him, knowing that even if you don't have everything you want right now, you already have everything you need. And that's a powerful place to live from.

Let's go back to what Paul wrote in Philippians 4:13: *"I can do all things through Christ who strengthens me."*This isn't just a motivational quote for tough times; it's the key to living in contentment. Paul's contentment came from knowing that his strength wasn't in his circumstances, but in Christ. No matter what came his way—plenty or poverty, abundance or lack—he was secure because his foundation was in Jesus.

As we move forward in our lives, let's make a decision today: to cultivate a spirit of gratitude, to rest in the peace of contentment, and to trust in God's provision. The more we thank God for what He's done, the more we'll see His hand in every detail of our lives. And as we do, we'll find that we have more than enough to live abundantly, no matter where we are or what we're facing.

So, let me leave you with this powerful quote: "*Gratitude turns what we have into enough, and contentment turns enough into more than we could ever ask for.*"

May you go forward in life knowing that God's blessings are overflowing, that His provision is perfect, and that in Him, you have everything you need.

## CHAPTER 8

# Serving Others

> **THE EXAMPLE OF JESUS – OUR ULTIMATE SERVANT**

Matthew 20:28 – *"Just as the Son of Man did not come to be served, but to serve, and to give His life as a ransom for many."*

When we think of success, many envision power, status, and authority. But Jesus flipped that idea on its head. He showed us a different path to greatness—a path of humility and service. Jesus, the Son of God, came not to be served but to serve. He didn't sit on a throne, expecting to be honored. Instead, He walked among the people, washed their feet, healed the sick, and ultimately gave His life for humanity.

Imagine the King of kings, the One who had all power and authority, choosing to humble Himself and serve. He didn't demand honor or recognition, and yet, His life made the greatest impact the world has ever seen. Jesus' legacy is not found in titles or accolades, but in His acts of love and service.

## Service is Love in Action

At its core, serving others is love in action. When we serve, we're putting the needs of others before our own. We're expressing the love of God in a tangible, meaningful way. Jesus didn't just talk about love; He demonstrated it through His actions. He loved the unlovable, touched the untouchable, and forgave the unforgivable. He served not just those who could repay Him, but also those who couldn't offer Him anything in return.

In the same way, when we serve others—whether it's through small, everyday acts of kindness or larger, sacrificial deeds—we are reflecting Christ's love. We are living out the calling that God has placed on our lives to love one another as He has loved us.

## A Life Changed by Service

Let me tell you a story about Mark, a businessman who was chasing success but felt an emptiness inside. He had all the money, the house, the luxury cars, but deep down, something was missing. One day, his church asked for volunteers to serve at a local homeless shelter. Reluctantly, Mark agreed to help.

At first, it felt awkward. Serving meals to people who had nothing felt so foreign to him. But as the night went on, Mark saw the smiles of those he served. He listened to their stories, and suddenly, the emptiness in his heart began to fade. He realized that in serving these individuals, he was serving God.

By the end of the night, Mark had found something far more valuable than wealth or material possessions—he found purpose. He went from being a man focused solely on his own success to a man passionate about making a difference in the lives of others. His life was forever changed, not by what he received, but by what he gave.

As we think about Jesus' example, we must ask ourselves: **How can I serve those around me?** What can I do to express God's love in action? When we follow Jesus' example of humility and service, we unlock a level of fulfillment and joy that cannot be found anywhere else.

Serving is more than just an obligation; it's a privilege. We get to be the hands and feet of Jesus in this world, touching lives and making an eternal impact. When we serve, we're not just changing the lives of others; we're transforming our own hearts in the process.

## THE HEART OF A SERVANT – SHIFTING OUR PERSPECTIVE

Galatians 5:13 – *"For you were called to freedom, brothers. Only do not use your freedom as an opportunity for the flesh, but through love serve one another."*

Service begins in the heart. To truly serve others, we first need to cultivate a servant's heart. This means shifting our mindset from 'What can I get?' to 'What can I give?' It's easy to focus on our own needs, ambitions, and desires, especially in a world that teaches us to chase after our own success. But the Bible calls us to a different way of living—one that places the needs of others before our own.

## Freedom to Serve

Galatians 5:13 reminds us that we have been given freedom through Christ, but that freedom isn't just for personal gain. It's not about living life solely for ourselves. God set us free so that we could use that freedom to serve one another in love. Think about that for a moment—your purpose is not found in serving yourself, but in serving others.

Serving others doesn't mean neglecting your own needs or dreams, but it's about recognizing that true joy and fulfillment come when we make a positive difference in someone else's life. The more we give of ourselves—our time, our talents, our resources—the more God multiplies blessings in our own lives.

## A Shift in Perspective

We often think that serving others will cost us something. We imagine it will take away from our own progress or success. But the truth is, when we serve, we don't lose; we gain. We gain perspective, purpose, and fulfillment. Our world expands as we open our eyes to the needs around us.

Take the story of Emily, for example. She worked long hours in a high-powered corporate job. Her focus was always on climbing the career ladder, but no matter how high she went, she felt a void. She had heard a sermon on the importance of serving others and decided to volunteer at a local children's hospital once a week.

At first, Emily thought her time spent volunteering was just a nice way to 'give back,' but soon, she realized that this was the most fulfilling part of her week. Interacting with those children, bringing them joy and comfort, gave her a sense of purpose that her job couldn't. The act of serving others brought her heart more peace and joy than any career achievement ever had.

**Serving in Every Season**

Sometimes we wait for the 'right time' to serve—when we have more free time, more money, or fewer responsibilities. But God calls us to serve in every season of life. Whether you're a student, a parent, a businessperson, or retired, you can find ways to serve right where you are. It doesn't have to be grand or extravagant; even small acts of kindness can make a big difference.

You don't have to wait until your life is 'perfect' to start serving. In fact, it's often through serving others that we experience breakthroughs in our own lives. When we focus on meeting the needs of others, God meets our needs in ways we never imagined.

Ask yourself, **Where can I shift my perspective to serve others? How can I use my freedom in Christ to bless those around me?** Remember, serving is not just a duty—it's an honor. God has placed unique gifts, talents, and resources in your life to be a blessing to others. The more we serve with a heart of love, the more we reflect the heart of Christ.

When we embrace the heart of a servant, we unlock a life of purpose, joy, and deep satisfaction. God uses our acts of service to transform not only the lives of those we help but also our own. True success in God's eyes comes from how well we love and serve those around us.

# THE EXAMPLE OF CHRIST – SERVING AS HE SERVED

Matthew 20:28 – *"Even as the Son of Man came not to be served but to serve, and to give his life as a ransom for many."*

If we want to understand the essence of service, we need look no further than Jesus Christ Himself. The very Son of God, who had all power and authority, chose to serve rather than be served. He set an example that radically redefined leadership and success.

## Christ's Approach to Service

From washing the feet of His disciples to feeding the hungry and healing the sick, Jesus embodied the spirit of servitude in every aspect of His ministry. He didn't just preach about love and service; He lived it out daily. He served those who were marginalized, the sick, and even those who would betray Him. Jesus knew that true greatness lies in humility and in the willingness to uplift others.

When Jesus washed the disciples' feet, He showed that no task is too menial for someone who wants to make a difference. In that culture, foot washing was a duty reserved for the lowest servant, yet He took on that role. By doing so, He demonstrated that serving others isn't about status or recognition; it's about love, compassion, and a heart willing to do whatever it takes to meet the needs of others.

## The Call to Follow His Example

As followers of Christ, we are called to emulate His example. We are not merely called to admire His actions from a distance; we are invited to participate in the same life of service. In a world that often promotes self-interest, Jesus invites us to take up our cross and serve others.

Consider the story of Thomas, a successful entrepreneur who seemed to have it all—wealth, status, and influence. However, he felt a growing emptiness inside. One day, he attended a church service where the pastor spoke about serving like Jesus. Inspired, Thomas decided to volunteer at a local shelter. He began serving meals, listening to stories, and building relationships with those in need.

Through this experience, Thomas found a new sense of purpose. He realized that his success was not measured by his bank account but by how he was impacting others. By following Christ's example of service, he discovered a deeper fulfillment that success alone could never provide.

## The Power of Sacrifice

True service often involves sacrifice. When we give of ourselves—our time, resources, and energy—we may find ourselves feeling drained or stretched thin. Yet, it is in those moments of sacrifice that we truly connect with the heart of God.

Jesus gave His life for us. He didn't hold anything back, and neither should we. Sacrificial service reflects the love and grace that He freely gives. When we choose to serve others, even when it's inconvenient or uncomfortable, we mirror the very character of Christ.

As you reflect on the example of Christ, ask yourself: **How can I serve like Jesus? What sacrifices can I make to bless others?** Serving is not always easy, but it is always worthwhile.

Remember, true greatness is found in humility and love. When we serve others, we are fulfilling our calling as disciples of Christ, and in doing so, we unlock the door to abundant life and true fulfillment.

When we embody the heart of a servant, we reflect Christ's love in a world that desperately needs it. As we continue on this journey of serving others, let's keep our eyes fixed on Him, our ultimate example. The more we serve, the more we become like Him, and the more we will experience the abundant life He has promised us.

## THE BLESSINGS OF SERVING OTHERS

Galatians 5:13 – *"For you were called to freedom, brothers. Only do not use your freedom as an opportunity for the flesh, but through love serve one another."*

When we talk about serving others, it's important to recognize that it's not just a duty or obligation; it's a pathway to countless blessings. Serving others can transform our lives and the lives of those around us. In fact, the act of service brings with it a profound sense of fulfillment, joy, and connection that nothing else can provide.

## THE JOY OF GIVING

One of the greatest blessings of serving others is the joy it brings. There's something incredibly rewarding about giving your time and energy to help someone else. Whether it's mentoring a young person, volunteering at a shelter, or simply lending a listening ear to a friend in need, the happiness we receive in return can be immeasurable.

Consider the story of Maria, a retired teacher who felt a void after leaving her job. She decided to volunteer at a local literacy program, helping adults learn to read. Initially, she thought she was there to help others, but what she found was an unexpected joy that filled her heart. Every smile, every "thank you," and every success story ignited a spark within her. Through her service, Maria discovered a renewed purpose and happiness that she hadn't felt in years.

## CREATING COMMUNITY AND CONNECTION

Serving others also fosters community. When we reach out to those in need, we build bridges of connection and understanding. In a world that often feels disconnected and divided, acts of service remind us of our shared humanity.

Think of a neighborhood that comes together to help a family in crisis. When individuals join forces to serve one another, barriers fall, and relationships grow. Serving cultivates empathy, compassion, and unity. It brings people from different backgrounds together with a common goal: to uplift and support one another.

## The Ripple Effect of Service

Moreover, the impact of serving others can create a ripple effect. One act of kindness can inspire others to do the same. When we serve selflessly, we ignite a spark in those around us. The person you help may go on to help someone else, creating a chain reaction of love and support that spreads far beyond what you could imagine.

Think about it: when you choose to serve, you're not just changing one life; you could be changing countless lives. Your service could be the catalyst for someone else's journey toward success, healing, or restoration.

## Serving with a Grateful Heart

The blessings of service are amplified when we serve with a grateful heart. Gratitude allows us to recognize the abundance we already have, making us more willing to share with others. When we approach service from a place of thankfulness, we shift our focus from what we lack to what we can give.

Reflect on the story of a local church that organized a community meal for those in need. The church members prepared food with love and gratitude, knowing that they were providing not just a meal but a sense of belonging. When people sat down together, the atmosphere was filled with joy and appreciation, creating lasting bonds between those serving and those being served.

As we reflect on the blessings that come from serving others, let's consider how we can be intentional in our service. Ask yourself: **What opportunities for service are present in my life right now? How can I be a blessing to someone today?**

When we embrace a life of service, we open ourselves to a world of joy, connection, and purpose. Let's remember that, as we serve, we are not only changing lives but also experiencing the rich blessings that flow from a heart committed to loving and serving others.

As we continue this journey together, let's embrace the calling to serve one another and watch as our lives—and the lives of those we touch—are transformed by love and kindness.

## Serving as a Reflection of Christ

Matthew 20:28 – *"Just as the Son of Man did not come to be served, but to serve, and to give His life as a ransom for many."*

To truly understand the essence of service, we must look to the ultimate example: Jesus Christ. In His time on Earth, He demonstrated that greatness is found in serving others, not in being served. His life was a living testament to humility, compassion, and selflessness.

## The Example of Christ's Service

From washing His disciples' feet to healing the sick, Jesus showed us that service isn't about status; it's about love and humility. He didn't shy away from the dirty work or the needs of the marginalized. Instead,

He actively sought out those who were suffering and in need.

For instance, in the Gospel of Mark, we see Jesus healing a leper—a task that would have made many people uncomfortable due to societal norms. But Jesus didn't let that stop Him. He reached out, touched the leper, and healed him (Mark 1:40-45). This act was not only a miracle but a powerful example of what it means to serve with love and compassion.

## Our Call to Serve Like Christ

As followers of Christ, we are called to emulate His example. Serving others is not just a good idea; it is a mandate for our lives. When we serve, we reflect Christ's love and character to the world. We demonstrate His grace, kindness, and compassion in a way that speaks louder than words ever could.

Let's think about how we can serve in our daily lives. It could be as simple as helping a neighbor with groceries, volunteering at a local charity, or even offering encouragement to someone who is struggling. Each of these acts, no matter how small, can be a reflection of Christ's heart for others.

## The Power of Humility in Service

Humility is a critical aspect of serving like Christ. It requires us to put aside our own desires and needs for the sake of others. This is not always easy, especially in a culture that often celebrates self-promotion and individualism.

However, when we choose humility, we align ourselves with God's purpose. James 4:10 reminds us, *"Humble yourselves before the Lord, and He will lift you up."* When we lower ourselves to lift others, God elevates us in His kingdom. He honors those who serve with a humble heart.

## Transforming Lives Through Service

Serving others can be a transformative experience for both the giver and the receiver. When we step into the shoes of those we serve, we gain a deeper understanding of their struggles and joys. This connection can lead to profound changes in our perspectives and attitudes.

Consider the story of John, a successful businessman who dedicated his weekends to serving meals at a local homeless shelter. Initially, he thought he was there to help others, but he quickly realized that the experience was changing him. Listening to the stories of those he served opened his eyes to the struggles people face every day. The more he served, the more compassion he felt in his heart.

Through his service, John found a new sense of purpose and fulfillment. He realized that the time spent serving others was far more rewarding than any business deal he could close. He discovered that true success is measured not by wealth or status but by the impact we have on the lives of those around us.

As we reflect on Jesus' example of service, let's ask ourselves: **How can I serve others in my community? What sacrifices am I willing to make to reflect Christ's love?**

When we serve others as Christ did, we become agents of change in the world. We embody His love, grace, and mercy, reminding those we serve that they are valued and cherished. Let's commit ourselves to a life of service, following in the footsteps of our Savior.

In doing so, we not only honor Him but also experience the joy and fulfillment that comes from living a life dedicated to serving others. Let's carry this spirit of service into every aspect of our lives, allowing it to transform us and those around us.

## THE REWARDS OF SERVING OTHERS

Galatians 6:9 – *"And let us not grow weary of doing good, for in due season we will reap, if we do not give up."*

When we think about serving others, we often focus on the immediate needs we are meeting or the tangible benefits of our actions. However, the rewards of service extend far beyond what we can see at the moment. God promises that when we commit ourselves to serving others, there are blessings waiting for us.

### The Principle of Reaping What You Sow

The Bible is clear about the principle of sowing and reaping. In Galatians 6:7, we read, *"Do not be deceived: God is not mocked, for whatever one sows, that will he also reap."* This principle applies to our acts of service. When we sow kindness, compassion, and selflessness, we will eventually reap a harvest of blessings in our own lives.

Think about it: every time you choose to serve someone—whether it's volunteering your time, offering a listening ear, or lending a helping hand—you are planting seeds of goodwill. And in God's perfect timing, those seeds will bear fruit. You may find that you receive encouragement when you need it most, unexpected opportunities arise, or relationships deepen in ways you hadn't anticipated.

## Unexpected Blessings

Sometimes, the blessings that come from serving others are not what we expect. We may not receive a material reward or recognition, but the impact on our hearts and the hearts of those we serve can be profound. For instance, consider a woman named Sarah who spent her weekends volunteering at a local shelter. Initially, she thought she was helping those in need, but she quickly discovered that her experiences there filled her with a joy and purpose she had been missing in her own life.

As Sarah poured into others, she also experienced emotional healing and newfound friendships. The gratitude she expressed to those she served came back to her tenfold, as they encouraged her and shared their stories of hope and resilience. This reciprocal relationship between serving and being served illustrates the beautiful cycle of giving.

## Heavenly Rewards

Moreover, the ultimate reward for serving others is found in the heavenly perspective. Matthew 25:40 reminds us, *"And the King will answer them, 'Truly, I say to you, as you did it to one of the least of these my brothers, you did it to me.'"* Every act of kindness is seen and honored by God. When we serve those who are marginalized or in need, we are serving Christ Himself.

In heaven, there will be a great celebration for every act of service we have performed in His name. These are not just fleeting moments; they have eternal significance. We will be rewarded not just for the big gestures but also for the small acts of kindness that might go unnoticed by the world.

## Serving Through Trials

Additionally, serving others during our own trials can lead to incredible breakthroughs. When we face challenges, it can be tempting to focus solely on our problems. Yet, when we reach out to help others, we shift our perspective and allow God to work through us.

There's a powerful story of a man named Tom who was going through a tough season in his life. He had lost his job and was feeling defeated. Instead of wallowing in self-pity, he decided to volunteer at a local food pantry. As he served those who were struggling, he began to feel a sense of purpose return to his life.

Through his service, Tom not only made a positive impact on the community, but he also found new friendships and connections that led to job opportunities he never expected. His willingness to serve during his own hardship opened doors that would lead him to a brighter future.

As we contemplate the rewards of serving others, let's remember that our efforts are not in vain. Every act of service counts, and God sees every one of them. Ask yourself: **What rewards am I seeking in my service? Am I looking for immediate recognition, or am I willing to trust God for the blessings that come in His perfect timing?**

Let us commit to a lifestyle of service, knowing that as we give of ourselves, we are sowing seeds that will reap an abundant harvest. In doing so, we'll experience the joy of serving and the incredible blessings that follow.

## SERVING WITH HUMILITY

Scripture: Philippians 2:3-4 – *"Do nothing out of selfish ambition or vain conceit. Rather, in humility value others above yourselves, not looking to your own interests but each of you to the interests of the others."*

One of the most beautiful aspects of serving others is the opportunity it gives us to practice humility. Serving isn't about seeking recognition or praise; it's about placing others' needs before our own and following the example of Jesus, who washed His disciples' feet, showing them that true greatness is found in humility.

## THE HEART OF A SERVANT

To serve with humility, we have to approach others with a genuine desire to help, not to be seen or celebrated. Sometimes, this means doing tasks that no one else wants to do, stepping into roles that may seem insignificant, or offering our time and energy without expecting anything in return.

When we serve with humility, we're imitating Christ's heart. Jesus didn't serve others with the intent of being honored—He did it out of love and compassion. He cared for the poor, healed the sick, and taught the truth, often without a large crowd to witness His acts. This is the essence of humility in service: helping others even when there's no applause, trusting that God sees what we do in secret and will reward us in His way.

## OVERCOMING PRIDE

Serving humbly also involves letting go of pride. Pride can be one of the biggest barriers to serving others effectively. When we're consumed with our own interests or worried about how others perceive us, we may hesitate to step out and help, fearing it might be seen as weakness or interfere with our own goals.

A powerful example is the story of a successful businessman named Mark, who decided to volunteer at a community center. Initially, Mark struggled with his pride. He felt overqualified and sometimes looked down on the small tasks assigned to him. But over time, he realized that serving others wasn't about his achievements or qualifications; it was about helping meet the needs around him.

As Mark let go of his pride, he discovered that the simple acts of serving meals, cleaning, and chatting with those in need were deeply fulfilling. He learned that service is not about what we bring to the table, but about the love and compassion we show. By embracing humility, Mark experienced a renewed sense of purpose and a deeper connection with God.

## VALUING OTHERS ABOVE OURSELVES

Another key to serving with humility is to value others above ourselves. This doesn't mean thinking less of ourselves but thinking more about how we can uplift others. When we see people through God's eyes, we recognize their worth and feel compelled to help.

In a world that often emphasizes competition, humility reminds us that success is not a race, but a journey we can take together. Serving with humility means we're not striving to be "the best," but seeking to bring out the best in others. It's an opportunity to show that we care more about people than accolades.

So, as you consider the role of humility in service, ask yourself: **How can I serve others with a humble heart? Am I willing to let go of pride and focus on the needs of those around me?** Let's remember that in God's kingdom, the greatest leaders are the ones who serve with humility and grace.

When we approach service from a place of humility, we not only honor God but also impact lives in ways that are deeply meaningful. Serving with humility is one of the purest forms of worship, reflecting God's love and drawing us closer to His heart.

## THE LASTING REWARDS OF SERVING OTHERS

Matthew 25:40 – *"The King will reply, 'Truly I tell you, whatever you did for one of the least of these brothers and sisters of mine, you did for me.'"*

Serving others isn't just a temporary act; it leaves an enduring mark, not only on the lives we touch but also on our own journey with God. Each act of service, no matter how small, builds into a legacy of love, faith, and compassion that transcends our lifetime. In God's kingdom, success isn't measured by material wealth or worldly achievements, but by the impact we make in the lives of others. When we serve others, we're sowing seeds that grow into blessings, sometimes in ways we may never fully see.

## SERVING WITH AN ETERNAL PERSPECTIVE

When we choose to serve with an eternal perspective, our focus shifts from what we can gain in this world to how we can contribute to God's work here on Earth. Every time we lend a hand, offer a kind word, or go out of our way to help, we're investing in something far greater than ourselves. We're building up treasures in heaven, where neither rust nor decay can touch them. Our acts of service become part of our eternal reward, cherished by God.

## A LEGACY OF LOVE

Imagine a life lived in service—a life filled with compassion, kindness, and selflessness. That's a life that echoes into eternity. When we leave this world, it won't be the accolades or possessions that people remember; it will be the love we poured out. The kindness shown, the burdens lifted, and the hearts touched by our presence will form the legacy we leave behind. Our service speaks volumes about the love of Christ, reflecting His grace and generosity to those around us.

## FINDING FULFILLMENT THROUGH SERVING OTHERS

As we close this chapter, remember that true fulfillment comes not from receiving, but from giving. Jesus Himself said that it is more blessed to give than to receive (Acts 20:35). Serving others allows us to experience the joy that flows from being part of something larger than ourselves. We find peace and satisfaction, knowing we've made a difference and brought light into someone's life.

Let's be intentional in our acts of service, allowing God to work through us to bring His love to the world. Look for opportunities each day to serve others with a joyful heart and an attitude of gratitude. Remember that every time you serve, you are serving Christ Himself.

In serving others, we find our greatest purpose and fulfillment. As you go forward, let this be your prayer: **Lord, help me to serve with a humble heart, to love**

**without limits, and to leave a legacy of kindness that honors You.**

In the end, our lives will be measured not by what we achieved for ourselves, but by what we gave of ourselves. When we serve others, we are fulfilling our highest calling and honoring the God who made us."

## CHAPTER 9

# Forgiveness and Letting Go

### UNDERSTANDING THE WEIGHT OF UNFORGIVENESS

Imagine, for a moment, carrying a backpack filled with stones. Every stone represents an offense, a hurt, or a betrayal you've experienced in life. Maybe it was a friend who let you down, a loved one who betrayed your trust, or even a colleague who spread lies about you. With each offense, you place another stone in that backpack. After a while, it becomes hard to move forward, doesn't it? You're weighed down, exhausted, and before long, that burden starts holding you back from the life God has in store for you.

This is what unforgiveness does to our spirit. It's a heavy load we carry, one that keeps us from experiencing the freedom and joy that God desires for us. When we cling to grudges, replay hurts in our minds, and let bitterness fester, we're only keeping ourselves captive. You see, unforgiveness isn't about punishing the person who hurt us; it's a form of punishment we inflict on ourselves. And if we're not careful, it will rob us of the peace, the purpose, and the power God has given us to fulfill our destiny.

The Bible warns us about this in Hebrews 12:15, which says, *"See to it that no one misses the grace of God and that no bitter root grows up to cause trouble and defile many."* Bitterness doesn't just impact our relationship with others; it keeps us from receiving God's grace fully. That bitterness becomes a root that digs deep into our hearts, turning into a stronghold that keeps us from the joy and success He has planned for us.

Unforgiveness is like drinking poison and expecting the other person to be harmed by it. It's holding onto a past wound, hoping it will bring you closure, but it only brings more pain. Jesus, our perfect example, showed us another way. He taught us to forgive—not seven times, but seventy times seven. He taught us to pray, "*Father, forgive them, for they know not what they do.*" When Jesus was on the cross, He didn't let bitterness take root. He released it. He forgave. And that forgiveness was His pathway to glory, just as it can be our pathway to freedom and success.

When we choose forgiveness, we choose to lighten our load. We make room for God's blessings, for His grace, and for the opportunities He wants to place in our lives. Maybe you've been holding onto some old hurts—people who wronged you years ago, memories that still sting, relationships that fell apart. Can I encourage you today? Don't let that pain hold you back any longer. Release it. Give it to God. Trust that He will bring justice in His perfect timing.

As we go through this chapter, let's open our hearts to God's healing touch. Let's make room in our souls to receive the peace, freedom, and success He's promised us. We weren't meant to carry the weight of unforgiveness; God's plan is for us to be light, free, and ready to run the race set before us.

## THE TRANSFORMATIVE POWER OF LETTING GO

Imagine stepping into a new season of your life, one where you're not weighed down by resentment or past disappointments. What if you could walk forward without the chains of anger or bitterness holding you back? That's what forgiveness does; it releases us into the freedom God intends for our lives. But sometimes, the hardest part isn't forgiving others—it's learning to forgive ourselves.

Many of us carry wounds not only from others but also from the mistakes we've made, the opportunities we've missed, or the times we fell short. We feel the weight of regret pressing on us, and we convince ourselves that God must be disappointed in us too. But let me tell you: our God isn't standing over us in condemnation. He's reaching out His hand in compassion, calling us forward into a new life.

Psalm 103:12 reminds us, *"As far as the east is from the west, so far has he removed our transgressions from us."* God doesn't hold our mistakes against us. He doesn't keep a record of wrongs. When we bring our burdens to Him, He wipes the slate clean. He calls us His beloved,

His chosen, His redeemed. If God Himself chooses to forgive us, who are we to hold onto shame or guilt?

Imagine how light we would feel if we accepted that same forgiveness for ourselves. It's like walking out of a prison cell you didn't realize you were in. Self-forgiveness isn't about excusing our actions or pretending they didn't happen; it's about releasing ourselves from the shame that God has already freed us from. When we let go of that guilt, we're opening the door for God's grace to flow more fully into our lives.

A man once shared a story about his journey of letting go. He had struggled for years to forgive himself for decisions he'd made in his youth. He'd built up a successful career and family, but in quiet moments, he felt the weight of past regrets hanging over him like a cloud. But one day, in prayer, he sensed God saying, *"Why are you carrying something I've already forgotten?"* It was as though chains fell from his heart. He realized that while he had been holding onto his past, God had already let it go. That day, he chose to forgive himself, and in doing so, he found a new level of peace and purpose.

Friend, if you're carrying regrets today, know that God doesn't want you to live under that shadow. He's calling you into the light, into freedom, into forgiveness. Every moment spent in shame is a moment we're not fully embracing the purpose God has for us. When we forgive ourselves, we align our perspective with God's. We see ourselves not through the lens of past mistakes but through the eyes of grace, potential, and purpose.

So, ask yourself: What would it look like to fully release that burden? What doors would open in your life if you chose to let go, to forgive, to walk in the freedom God has promised?

## EMBRACING FORGIVENESS AS A DAILY PRACTICE

In a world where it's all too easy to accumulate small hurts and disappointments, forgiveness can't be a one-time decision; it has to become a way of life. It's a choice we make daily to release anger, disappointment, and resentment, allowing God's peace to fill those spaces instead. When we commit to a lifestyle of forgiveness, we're choosing to keep our hearts open, our spirits light, and our paths unencumbered by bitterness.

Think about it—how often do we let the small offenses of the day pile up in our hearts? Maybe a friend overlooked a promise, a family member made a cutting remark, or a colleague didn't give credit where it was due. Over time, these little things can build up, creating walls within us that separate us from others and even from God. But imagine how different life could be if we chose to let go each day, releasing our frustrations to God and choosing peace over pain.

Ephesians 4:32 encourages us, saying, *"Be kind and compassionate to one another, forgiving each other, just as in Christ God forgave you."* This isn't just a suggestion; it's an invitation to live freely and fully. When we forgive others, we're not excusing their actions; we're releasing ourselves from the control that bitterness can hold over our lives. Forgiveness liberates us—it's a gift we give ourselves even as we extend grace to others.

A woman shared a powerful testimony about how this practice transformed her life. For years, she carried resentment toward a family member who had hurt her deeply. Every interaction was tense, every family gathering filled with unspoken hostility. She realized this pain was stealing her joy, robbing her of peace.

One day, in prayer, she felt God prompting her to forgive, not just once but to commit to a daily choice to release that anger. She began praying every morning, asking God to help her let go and bless that family member. Over time, her heart softened, and so did the relationship. What she once thought was impossible became a reality because she chose forgiveness as a lifestyle.

Forgiveness isn't about forgetting; it's about choosing freedom. It's deciding that your peace and joy are more valuable than holding onto a grudge. As we forgive, we also open the door for God to work miracles in our relationships, to mend what was broken, and to renew what felt lost.

Friend, consider this: what would it look like if forgiveness became your daily habit? If you could start each day with a heart free from resentment, ready to embrace the fullness of God's blessings? That's the invitation before us—to let go, to forgive, and to embrace the freedom God offers.

In choosing forgiveness, we're choosing a life where love, not resentment, leads the way. We're declaring that no hurt is too great for God's healing and that every day is an opportunity to walk in the freedom Christ has already won for us. It's in this daily release, this conscious choice, that we find lasting peace and true success in God's eyes.

## FORGIVING YOURSELF TO EMBRACE GOD'S PLAN

One of the hardest, yet most essential, types of forgiveness is forgiving ourselves. So many of us are walking around with regrets and shame that weigh heavily on our hearts. Maybe it's a mistake from the past, a choice we wish we hadn't made, or a moment we would give anything to redo. But holding onto guilt can be just as destructive as holding onto anger toward someone else.

When we cling to guilt, we're essentially saying that our mistakes are bigger than God's mercy. But here's the truth: nothing you've done, no matter how big or small, can ever separate you from the love of God. In Romans 8:38-39, we're reminded that nothing *"will be able to separate us from the love of God that is in Christ Jesus our Lord."* That includes our past mistakes, our regrets, and even our failures. God's love and grace cover it all.

Imagine carrying a heavy backpack everywhere you go. It's filled with stones of regret, shame, and self-blame. Every day, that weight makes it harder to walk the path God has set before you. But the moment you choose to forgive yourself, you're taking off that backpack, laying it at the feet of Jesus, and allowing Him to carry the load. It's in that act of release that you find the freedom to step forward into God's plan for your life.

A young man once shared a powerful story of his own journey toward self-forgiveness. Years ago, he made some choices that he knew were wrong, choices that hurt people he loved and left him feeling like he could never make things right. He spent years feeling undeserving of God's love, believing that he had fallen too far. But one day, he heard a message about God's mercy and realized he'd been carrying a burden that wasn't his to bear. He began to pray, asking God to help him forgive himself and trust in His forgiveness. It didn't happen overnight, but day by day, he felt the weight lift. Today, he's using his experiences to help others, finding purpose in the very places he once felt broken.

Psalm 103:12 tells us, *"As far as the east is from the west, so far has he removed our transgressions from us."* If God has forgiven you, then who are you not to forgive yourself? Embracing this truth means seeing yourself through God's eyes—as redeemed, renewed, and ready to fulfill His calling.

When we forgive ourselves, we're saying yes to God's grace and allowing Him to reshape our lives, no matter where we've been. It's a bold act of faith to trust that God's plans for us are still good, even when we've stumbled. It's choosing to believe that every mistake, every regret, is a part of our story that God can use for His glory.

So let go of that burden. Lay down the regret. Embrace God's love fully, and let it wash over every broken place in your heart. When you do, you'll find yourself lighter, freer, and ready to walk boldly into the future God has for you. Friend, if God can forgive you, then it's time for you to forgive yourself. Because God's plans are too big, too beautiful, for you to stay bound by what's already been forgiven.

## THE POWER OF FORGIVENESS IN RELATIONSHIPS

Forgiveness isn't just a personal journey; it profoundly impacts our relationships with others. Every interaction we have is an opportunity to reflect God's love and grace. But when we hold onto resentment and bitterness, we create barriers that can hinder our ability to connect meaningfully with those around us.

Consider the story of Joseph in the Bible. Sold into slavery by his brothers, falsely accused, and thrown into prison, Joseph faced immense betrayal. Yet, when he finally stood before his brothers years later, he didn't seek revenge. Instead, he offered forgiveness and love, saying in Genesis 50:20, *"You intended to harm me, but God intended it for good."* Joseph understood that holding onto grudges would only keep him chained to his past, preventing him from stepping into the fullness of God's plan for his life.

When we choose to forgive, we are releasing ourselves from the weight of anger and bitterness. We're also opening the door for healing and restoration in our relationships. Forgiveness allows us to build stronger connections, rooted in love rather than pain. It's about recognizing our shared humanity and understanding that we all make mistakes.

Let's take a moment to reflect on the relationships in our lives. Are there wounds that need healing? Are there past grievances that still linger in your heart? Perhaps it's a friend who betrayed you, a family member who hurt you, or even a colleague who crossed a line. Whatever it may be, know that the power of forgiveness can transform those relationships.

Forgiveness doesn't mean we condone hurtful actions. It doesn't mean we forget what happened or dismiss the pain. Rather, it's a conscious decision to let go of the past so we can create a healthier future. It's a gift we give not only to others but also to ourselves. As Ephesians 4:32 encourages us, *"Be kind to one another, tenderhearted, forgiving one another, as God in Christ forgave you."*

When we embody forgiveness, we reflect God's heart. We become vessels of His grace, showing others that redemption is possible, even in the messiest of circumstances. This doesn't mean the journey of forgiveness will always be easy or immediate.

Sometimes, it requires daily commitment to release our hurt and seek reconciliation.

I recall a testimony of a woman who had endured a painful divorce. For years, she harbored resentment towards her ex-husband, feeling wronged and betrayed. It was only when she began to pray for him—truly pray, seeking God's best for his life—that she felt a shift in her heart. She realized that her bitterness was only harming herself, holding her back from experiencing joy and peace. As she began to forgive, she found the freedom to move forward, embracing new relationships without the burden of her past.

Forgiveness can pave the way for healing not just in our hearts, but also in the lives of those around us. When we extend grace, we create an atmosphere of love, understanding, and support. It's a ripple effect that starts with us and can touch the lives of countless others.

As you reflect on this, remember that God is always with you. He's walking alongside you, guiding you through the process of forgiveness. He sees the pain, the heartache, and the struggles, and He longs to help you release them into His capable hands. Lean on

Him as you navigate these relationships. Let His love empower you to forgive and experience the peace that comes from letting go.

In the words of Colossians 3:13, *"Bear with each other and forgive one another if any of you has a grievance against someone. Forgive as the Lord forgave you."* This is a divine invitation to embrace the power of forgiveness, not just as an act of obedience, but as a pathway to deeper relationships and a more profound understanding of God's love.

## RELEASING THE PAST TO EMBRACE THE FUTURE

To truly put God first in our relationships, we must learn to release the past and embrace the future that He has in store for us. Holding onto past hurts can cloud our judgment and prevent us from seeing the beautiful opportunities God has laid out before us. It's like trying to drive a car while looking in the rearview mirror—we miss the beauty of the road ahead!

Let's think about the Israelites as they wandered in the desert. They were trapped in a cycle of longing for the past, often reminiscing about their time in Egypt, despite it being a place of bondage. In Numbers 11:5, they lamented, *"We remember the fish we ate in Egypt at no cost—also the cucumbers, melons, leeks, onions, and garlic."* They were so focused on what they had left behind that they missed the miraculous provision God was offering in the present.

Isn't that how we sometimes are? We cling to our memories, both good and bad, allowing them to dictate our present and future. But God wants us to step out of that old mindset. He's calling us to trust Him and to move forward, unshackled by the chains of past mistakes, failures, and grievances. He's ready to do something new in your life!

When we make the conscious choice to release the past, we're saying yes to God's promise of a brighter future. It requires courage and a willingness to let go of our comfort zones. But the reward is priceless: we can experience the joy of new beginnings. In Isaiah 43:18-19, God encourages us, saying, *"Forget the former things; do not dwell on the past. See, I am doing a new thing! Now it springs up; do you not perceive it?"*

This isn't just a command; it's an invitation to look forward with anticipation. When we let go of the past, we make room for God's abundant blessings. We allow ourselves to be vessels for His love and grace, enabling us to build meaningful relationships rooted in His promises.

Let's consider the story of a man who faced significant setbacks in his career. After being laid off, he felt defeated and overwhelmed by thoughts of failure. He spent countless nights reflecting on what went wrong, replaying scenarios in his mind. But one day, he felt a nudge from God, urging him to release the hurt and step into a new season. He took a leap of faith, updating his resume and applying for new positions with a renewed spirit.

Through his willingness to let go of the past, he not only found a new job but also discovered a passion he never knew existed. This new opportunity allowed him to use his gifts in ways he had never imagined, ultimately leading to a more fulfilling career. God had a plan for him all along; he just needed to trust and release his past to embrace it.

The same can happen for us! When we decide to release our past grievances, we open ourselves to new possibilities and relationships. We begin to view others through a lens of grace, recognizing that everyone has their battles. This shift in perspective can heal wounds and foster deeper connections.

It's important to understand that letting go of the past doesn't mean forgetting. It's about choosing not to let those memories dictate our present actions or relationships. It's about taking the lessons learned and using them to grow stronger and wiser. As we navigate the process of releasing past hurts, we can lean on God for strength and guidance.

Prayer can be a powerful tool in this process. By bringing our past grievances before God, we allow Him to work in our hearts. We can ask for healing, strength, and the ability to forgive those who have hurt us. Remember that Philippians 4:6-7 reminds us to bring our requests to God, and He will provide us with peace that transcends understanding.

As you go on this journey of releasing the past, invite God into your heart. Ask Him to help you let go of what no longer serves you. Trust that He is preparing something beautiful just for you. The more you embrace His love and grace, the more you will be able to open yourself up to the incredible plans He has laid out ahead.

So today, let's commit to putting God first in our relationships by choosing to release the past and embrace the new things He is doing in our lives. The journey may not always be easy, but it will be rewarding as we walk hand in hand with our Creator.

## BUILDING HEALTHY BOUNDARIES

As we put God first in our relationships, it is essential to establish healthy boundaries that foster respect, love, and mutual growth. Boundaries are not walls that shut others out; instead, they are protective barriers that allow us to maintain our values and emotional well-being while engaging meaningfully with others. When we draw boundaries grounded in God's principles, we create an environment where relationships can flourish.

In Proverbs 25:28, we are reminded, *"Like a city whose walls are broken through is a person who lacks self-control."* Boundaries act as our walls, helping us guard our hearts and prevent toxic dynamics from entering our relationships. Without them, we risk being overwhelmed by negativity or disrespect from those around us.

Consider a young woman named Sarah, who was always willing to help others at her own expense. She would cancel plans, ignore her needs, and stretch herself thin to accommodate everyone else. Initially, this seemed noble, but over time, Sarah found herself exhausted and unappreciated. It was in a moment of prayer that she felt God urging her to reevaluate her relationships. She realized she needed to set clear boundaries to protect her well-being while still being there for others.

As Sarah began to establish her boundaries, she communicated openly with her friends and family about her limits. Instead of feeling guilty for saying no, she found freedom in prioritizing her own needs. In doing so, she not only honored herself but also cultivated deeper, more respectful relationships where everyone's needs were considered. Setting boundaries allowed her to create space for God's love to flow more freely in her life.

We must understand that boundaries are a reflection of our self-worth and the love we have for ourselves as

God loves us. God calls us to care for our well-being, and establishing boundaries is part of that self-care. This is echoed in 1 Corinthians 6:19-20, where Paul reminds us that our bodies are temples of the Holy Spirit, urging us to honor God with our lives.

When we set boundaries, we communicate our values and expectations to others, fostering relationships built on mutual respect. Boundaries also protect us from potential manipulation or abuse, ensuring we engage with others from a place of strength. It's essential to remember that healthy boundaries can take time to establish and may require ongoing communication.

When we prioritize God in our relationships, we seek His guidance in defining our boundaries. We can ask ourselves:

- What are my non-negotiables?
- How can I communicate my needs without guilt?
- Am I surrounding myself with people who uplift and encourage me?

Through prayer and reflection, we can align our boundaries with God's desires for our relationships.

This may mean distancing ourselves from toxic influences or choosing to invest more time in relationships that inspire us.

As we establish these boundaries, it's vital to remain flexible and open to discussions. Healthy relationships are dynamic and require ongoing adjustments as circumstances change. It's about finding that balance where both parties feel valued and respected.

Ephesians 4:15 encourages us to *"speak the truth in love."* When we communicate our boundaries, it's essential to do so with kindness and clarity. Rather than approaching the conversation with defensiveness, let's present our boundaries as an opportunity for growth. Sharing our needs can strengthen bonds and foster understanding.

As we prioritize God in our relationships, let's remember that boundaries are not barriers but rather a means to nurture healthy connections. By setting limits, we create an environment where love, trust, and respect can flourish. Our relationships should reflect the love of Christ, which is patient, kind, and respectful.

We can also model healthy boundaries for others. By demonstrating how to establish and respect limits, we create a culture of mutual care in our relationships. As others witness our commitment to putting God first and honoring our needs, they may be inspired to do the same.

## CULTIVATING A SPIRIT OF FORGIVENESS

As we navigate our relationships with a God-first mindset, we must also cultivate a spirit of forgiveness. Forgiveness is one of the most profound gifts we can offer ourselves and others. It frees us from the burden of resentment and paves the way for healing and restoration. When we choose to forgive, we are not only obeying God's command but also aligning ourselves with His heart, which desires reconciliation and love.

In Ephesians 4:32, we are instructed, *"Be kind and compassionate to one another, forgiving each other, just as in Christ God forgave you."* This powerful verse reminds us that our ability to forgive is rooted in the forgiveness we have received through Christ. Just as

He extended grace to us, we are called to extend grace to others.

Let's consider the story of a man named David. David had a close friend who betrayed him in a significant way, causing him deep pain and heartache. For years, David held onto bitterness and anger, allowing it to affect his relationships and emotional well-being. One day, after reflecting on his struggles, he decided to take the courageous step of forgiveness.

In prayer, David sought God's help to release his anger and embrace a heart of compassion. He recognized that holding onto the past was preventing him from fully experiencing the joy and peace that God desired for him. Through the process of forgiveness, David discovered a renewed sense of freedom. Not only did his relationship with his friend improve, but he also found healing within himself.

Forgiveness is not always easy; it requires vulnerability and a willingness to let go of our hurts. It may involve confronting painful memories and choosing to see others through the lens of God's love. But when we forgive, we break the chains of bitterness and open our hearts to God's transformative power.

In Matthew 6:14-15, Jesus teaches, *"For if you forgive other people when they sin against you, your heavenly Father will also forgive you. But if you do not forgive others their sins, your Father will not forgive your sins."* This stark reminder emphasizes the importance of forgiveness in our relationship with God. We cannot expect to experience His grace fully if we are unwilling to extend that grace to others.

Forgiveness does not mean that we condone or forget the wrongs done to us. Instead, it is a conscious choice to release the hold that those offenses have on our hearts. It allows us to reclaim our peace and prevents the wounds from defining our relationships.

When we put God first, we invite His spirit of forgiveness into our lives. This may involve daily prayers asking for strength to forgive those who have hurt us and the grace to let go of our grudges. We can also meditate on scriptures that reinforce our commitment to forgiveness.

Consider reflecting on Colossians 3:13, which states, *"Bear with each other and forgive one another if any of you has a grievance against someone. Forgive as the Lord forgave you."* This verse serves as a reminder that forgiveness is not a one-time act but a continual practice. Each day offers us opportunities to forgive and extend grace to ourselves and others.

Forgiveness also nurtures a spirit of humility. When we acknowledge our own flaws and the forgiveness we've received, it becomes easier to extend that same grace to others. Humility opens our hearts to compassion, allowing us to see others as imperfect beings on their own journeys.

As we embrace forgiveness in our relationships, we must also remember to forgive ourselves. Sometimes, the hardest person to forgive is ourselves. We may grapple with guilt, shame, or regret for past actions. But as Romans 8:1 assures us, *"Therefore, there is now no condemnation for those who are in Christ Jesus."* Embracing God's forgiveness for our mistakes empowers us to move forward, live boldly, and love authentically.

In conclusion, cultivating a spirit of forgiveness is crucial as we put God first in our relationships. It liberates us from the weight of bitterness and allows us to experience the fullness of His love. By choosing to forgive, we align ourselves with God's heart and open ourselves to healing and restoration.

May we commit to embracing forgiveness in our lives, both for ourselves and for those who have wronged us. Trust in God's power to transform your heart and relationships as you walk in the freedom of forgiveness.

CHAPTER 10

# Embracing Change and Growth

Change is an inevitable part of life, a constant that we can count on through every season. Just as the seasons transition from the vibrant hues of spring to the quiet stillness of winter, our lives undergo transformations that shape who we are meant to become. But here's the beautiful truth: when we put God first, we are not merely enduring these changes—we are embracing them. We begin to see that every shift in our lives is a divine opportunity, a stepping stone toward growth that God has laid out for us.

In Isaiah 43:19, God says, *"See, I am doing a new thing! Now it springs up; do you not perceive it?"* This verse encapsulates the essence of change: God is always at work, crafting new paths and fresh beginnings for us. When we acknowledge that God is orchestrating our lives, we can face change not with fear but with faith.

Every time we find ourselves at a crossroads—be it in our careers, relationships, or personal journeys—we are being called to change. This is not just a whim; it's God's way of moving us toward His greater purpose. Sometimes, change can feel overwhelming, daunting even. We may question the decisions we've made, the paths we've taken, or the relationships we've fostered. Yet, it is often in these moments of uncertainty that God's voice shines the brightest. He whispers to us in our confusion, assuring us that He is in control.

## UNDERSTANDING CHANGE THROUGH A BIBLICAL LENS

### Biblical Examples of Change

Throughout Scripture, we encounter numerous individuals who faced monumental changes and the lessons we can learn from their journeys. For instance, consider Abraham, who was called to leave his homeland and venture into the unknown (Genesis 12:1-3). Abraham trusted God's promise, and through his obedience, he became the father of many nations. His willingness to embrace change was not just a personal journey; it was pivotal for the fulfillment of God's covenant.

Another powerful example is Joseph, who endured significant hardship—betrayal by his brothers, slavery, and imprisonment—before being elevated to a position of great authority in Egypt (Genesis 37-50). Joseph's story reminds us that God can turn our trials into triumphs, shaping our character and preparing us for the destiny He has planned.

These biblical narratives highlight that change is often accompanied by challenges. Yet, they also underscore the truth that God's purpose is at work, even when we cannot see it. As we navigate our own transitions, we can draw strength from these examples, knowing that God has a plan for our lives, just as He did for Abraham and Joseph.

## The Role of Trust in Change

When facing change, our trust in God is paramount. Proverbs 3:5-6 encourages us to *"Trust in the Lord with all your heart and lean not on your own understanding; in all your ways acknowledge Him, and He will make your paths straight."* This scripture serves as a guiding principle, reminding us that our limited perspective can hinder us from recognizing God's infinite wisdom.

Trusting God during times of transition requires a shift in our mindset. Instead of clinging to our comfort zones, we must be willing to release our fears and uncertainties to Him. This surrender is not passive; it is an active choice to believe that God is orchestrating every detail of our lives. When we trust Him fully, we open ourselves to the possibilities that change can bring, allowing His divine plan to unfold in ways we never imagined.

## The Power of Prayer in Navigating Change

In times of change, prayer becomes our lifeline. Philippians 4:6-7 reminds us to *"not be anxious about anything, but in every situation, by prayer and petition, with thanksgiving, present your requests to God."* When we communicate with God, we invite Him into our circumstances, seeking His guidance and wisdom.

Prayer is a powerful tool that can help us find clarity amidst confusion. It allows us to align our desires with God's will, ensuring that we are on the right path. As we pray, we cultivate a deeper relationship with God, fostering a sense of peace and assurance that He is with us every step of the way.

## Embracing a Growth Mindset

Adopting a growth mindset is essential for thriving amidst change. Rather than viewing obstacles as setbacks, we can see them as opportunities for growth. Romans 5:3-5 teaches us that *"suffering produces perseverance; perseverance, character; and character, hope."* Each challenge we face has the potential to refine us, building resilience and fortitude.

As we shift our focus from fear to growth, we begin to view change not as something to dread, but as a chance to evolve. Embracing a growth mindset encourages us to seek knowledge, learn from our experiences, and develop the skills necessary to navigate life's transitions. This proactive approach empowers us to take ownership of our journeys, trusting that God is molding us into the individuals He created us to be.

## Practicing Gratitude during Change

During times of transition, it can be easy to focus on what we are losing or what feels uncertain. However, practicing an attitude of gratitude can transform our perspective. 1 Thessalonians 5:18 encourages us to *"give thanks in all circumstances; for this is God's will for you in Christ Jesus."* Gratitude shifts our focus from our difficulties to the blessings we still possess.

When we practice gratitude, we acknowledge God's faithfulness and provision in our lives. This acknowledgment can fortify our spirits, reminding us that even in the midst of change, we have much to be thankful for. It helps us to maintain a positive outlook and find joy in the journey, regardless of the challenges we face.

## PREPARING FOR CHANGE WITH FAITH AND INTENTIONALITY

These are the ways to prepare for change with faith:

## Identifying Areas of Change

Before we can fully embrace change, it's essential to identify the specific areas of our lives that may need transformation. This could involve personal growth, career transitions, or even relational shifts. Reflecting on these areas can be both enlightening and empowering. The act of recognizing where change is needed often serves as the first step toward growth.

Consider the example of the Israelites as they prepared to enter the Promised Land. They had to confront their fears and doubts, letting go of their past to embrace a new future (Joshua 1:1-9). Similarly, we must assess our current situations and identify where God may be calling us to step out in faith. This intentionality allows us to focus our prayers and actions toward specific goals, aligning our steps with His purpose.

## Seeking God's Guidance

As we identify areas for change, seeking God's guidance is crucial. James 1:5 encourages us to *"ask God for wisdom, who gives generously to all without finding fault."* This verse reassures us that God is ready and willing to provide the insight we need to navigate our transitions.

When seeking guidance, consider establishing a regular routine of prayer and meditation. Create a space where you can quiet your mind and listen for God's voice. Journaling can also be a powerful practice, allowing you to document your thoughts, prayers, and the insights you receive. This habit not only helps you stay focused but also reveals God's faithfulness over time as you reflect on how He has directed your path.

**Setting Intentional Goals**

Once we have clarity on the changes we desire and have sought God's guidance, the next step is to set intentional goals. Setting specific, measurable, achievable, relevant, and time-bound (SMART) goals helps us create a roadmap for our transitions. Proverbs 16:3 reminds us to *"commit to the Lord whatever you do, and He will establish your plans."*

These goals should align with God's will for our lives, incorporating the lessons we've learned through prayer and reflection. Whether it's pursuing a new career, improving relationships, or deepening our spiritual walk, intentional goal-setting will guide our actions and keep us focused on our desired outcomes.

## Being a Part of a Supportive Community

Navigating change is often challenging, but we don't have to do it alone. Surrounding ourselves with a supportive community can provide encouragement, accountability, and wisdom. Hebrews 10:24-25 instructs us to *"consider how we may spur one another on toward love and good deeds, not giving up meeting together."*

Engage with your church community, participate in small groups, or find a mentor who can guide you through your journey. Sharing your goals with others not only fosters accountability but also invites others to support you in prayer and encouragement. Remember, you are part of the body of Christ, and together, you can lift each other up as you embrace the changes that lie ahead.

## Embracing Flexibility and Adaptability

While it's important to have goals, we must also remain flexible and adaptable. Life is unpredictable, and the path to our desired change may not always unfold as planned. Isaiah 55:8-9 reminds us that *"for my thoughts are not your thoughts, neither are your ways my ways."* This scripture invites us to trust in God's timing and methods, even when they differ from our own expectations.

Embracing flexibility means being open to new opportunities and adjusting our plans as needed. Sometimes, God leads us down paths we didn't anticipate, but these detours can often lead to greater blessings. By remaining adaptable, we cultivate resilience and a willingness to embrace the journey God has laid out for us.

## Taking Action Steps

Change requires action. Once we have identified our goals and established a supportive network, it's time to take actionable steps toward our desired transformation. These steps don't have to be monumental; even small, consistent actions can lead to significant progress over time.

For instance, if you're seeking to enhance your skills for a new career, consider enrolling in a course or seeking out workshops. If your goal is to strengthen relationships, schedule regular time to connect with loved ones. Remember, Proverbs 13:4 states that *"the soul of the sluggard craves and gets nothing, but the soul of the diligent is richly supplied."* Diligence in our efforts can bring forth the fruits of change.

## Celebrating Small Victories

As you take steps toward change, it's important to celebrate small victories along the way. Each achievement, no matter how minor, is a testament to your commitment and growth. Celebrating these moments not only boosts your morale but also serves as a reminder of God's faithfulness in your journey.

In the words of the psalmist, *"This is the day that the Lord has made; let us rejoice and be glad in it"* (Psalm 118:24). Taking time to reflect on your progress encourages gratitude and reinforces your belief in God's guiding hand. Share your victories with your community to inspire and uplift others as they navigate their own changes.

As we conclude this chapter on preparing for change, let us remember to walk in faith and confidence. God has equipped us with everything we need to navigate life's transitions. Philippians 4:13 affirms, *"I can do all things through Christ who strengthens me."*

This scripture serves as a powerful reminder that our strength comes not from ourselves but from God.

Embrace the changes ahead with the assurance that God is leading you. Trust in His ability to guide your steps, and step forward with boldness. Each new challenge is an opportunity for growth, and with God at the helm, you can approach every situation with courage and hope. Let this journey of transformation draw you closer to God, deepening your relationship with Him as you navigate the beautiful and intricate tapestry of change in your life.

## CONCLUSION

# The Key to Lasting Success

As we bring this journey to a close, it's vital to reflect on the core principles that have guided our exploration of putting God first. Each chapter has illuminated the importance of aligning our lives with God's will, reminding us that true success is not measured by earthly standards but by our relationship with Him. We have seen that by prioritizing God, we set the foundation for a life filled with faith, purpose, and abundance.

Throughout this book, we have learned that faith and trust in God form the bedrock of our success. Hebrews

11:1 teaches us that faith is the assurance of things hoped for, the conviction of things not seen. When we place our trust in God, we open the door to His divine guidance, enabling us to navigate life's challenges with confidence. This faith is further reinforced through the power of prayer, as outlined in Philippians 4:6-7, where we are encouraged to bring our requests before God, allowing His peace to guard our hearts and minds.

Integrity and honesty are paramount in all dealings. As emphasized in Proverbs 10:9, walking in integrity leads to security, while dishonest paths result in destruction. By committing to uphold these values, we cultivate trust in our relationships, both personal and professional, and we reflect God's character to those around us.

Hard work and diligence also play significant roles in our success. As Colossians 3:23-24 urges us, whatever we do should be done wholeheartedly, as working for the Lord. This commitment not only glorifies God but also positions us to reap the rewards of our efforts in His timing.

Patience and perseverance are necessary as we face trials and delays. James 1:3-4 encourages us to see the testing of our faith as an opportunity for growth, leading to maturity and completeness. By embracing patience, we align ourselves with God's timing, ensuring that we are prepared to receive the blessings He has in store for us.

Wisdom and discernment, as highlighted in James 1:5, equip us to make choices that honor God. When we seek His guidance, we gain clarity in our decision-making, leading us toward a future filled with purpose and fulfillment.

Gratitude and contentment are transformative practices that keep our hearts focused on God's goodness. As we cultivate a spirit of thankfulness, we shift our perspective from what we lack to the blessings we possess, fostering joy in every season of life.

Moreover, serving others is a pathway to success in God's eyes, as emphasized in Matthew 20:28. By embodying a servant heart, we reflect Christ's love and fulfill our calling to be agents of change in our communities.

The chapter on forgiveness and humility reinforce the idea that true success requires us to let go of past hurts and pride. Holding onto resentment only hinders our growth, while humility and obedience position us to receive God's favor and guidance. James 4:10 reminds us that when we humble ourselves before the Lord, He will lift us up, paving the way for blessings beyond our comprehension.

In closing, remember the words of Joshua 1:9: "*Have I not commanded you? Be strong and courageous. Do not be afraid; do not be discouraged, for the Lord your God will be with you wherever you go.*" As you continue on your journey, keep God first in every aspect of your life. Trust that as you seek Him and put His principles into practice, you will experience a profound transformation, leading to lasting success that reflects His glory.

May your commitment to putting God first be the guiding light in all your endeavors, and may His peace and blessings overflow in your life as you walk in faith.

## END WITH THIS PRAYER: A PRAYER FOR GUIDANCE AND STRENGTH

*"Heavenly Father, we come before You with grateful hearts, acknowledging Your goodness and faithfulness. Thank You for guiding us through this journey of understanding the importance of putting You first in our lives. Help us to carry these truths into our daily walk, trusting that when we seek You, we will find the strength and direction we need.*

*Lord, instill in us a spirit of faith and trust that fuels our actions. Teach us to pray diligently, to act with integrity, and to work hard as unto You. May we embrace patience and wisdom in our decisions, recognizing that Your timing is perfect.*

*Help us to serve others with joy and gratitude, reflecting Your love in our communities. Let us forgive those who have wronged us, freeing our hearts from bitterness and resentment. And may we walk in humility and obedience, knowing that true success is found in surrendering our lives to Your will.*

*Guide us each day, Lord, and remind us that You are always with us. Fill us with Your peace and courage as we take steps of faith into the future You have for us. We declare that with You by our side, we can overcome any obstacle and achieve the success that brings glory to Your name.*

*In Jesus' name, we pray. Amen."*

www.ingramcontent.com/pod-product-compliance
Lightning Source LLC
LaVergne TN
LVHW012244070526
838201LV00090B/121